# A Day in May

## Colin Murphy

### with Charlie Bird

*methuen* | drama
LONDON • NEW YORK • OXFORD • NEW DELHI • SYDNEY

METHUEN DRAMA
Bloomsbury Publishing Plc
50 Bedford Square, London, WC1B 3DP, UK
1385 Broadway, New York, NY 10018, USA
29 Earlsfort Terrace, Dublin 2, Ireland

BLOOMSBURY, METHUEN DRAMA and the Methuen
Drama logo are trademarks of Bloomsbury Publishing Plc

First published in Great Britain 2022

A catalogue record for this book is available from the British Library.

A catalog record for this book is available from the Library of Congress.

ISBN: PB: 978-1-3503-6969-6
ePDF: 978-1-3503-6970-2
eBook: 978-1-3503-6971-9

Series: Modern Plays

Typeset by Mark Heslington Ltd, Scarborough, North Yorkshire

To find out more about our authors and books visit
www.bloomsbury.com and sign up for our newsletters.

## Author's note

This play is, to a large extent, not in my words. It is based on a series of interviews conducted by Charlie Bird, many of which were separately collected in the book *A Day in May*, edited by Kevin Rafter. Amongst those whose stories appear are: Jenny Blake, Gavin and Sabina Brennan, Síona Cahill, June Hamill, Will Keane, Kathleen and Noel Sharkey, Steven Sharpe, Brian Sheehan and Nuala Ward. Some of Charlie's interviewees preferred to remain anonymous; to allow for this and for artistic licence, all names in the play have been changed. A fuller account of my sources is in the afterword.

Colin Murphy
October 2022

## A note from Charlie Bird

Despite my diagnosis of a terminal illness in October 2021, I have had many amazing things happening for me, including the success of #climbwithcharlie, which raised over €3 million for Pieta and the Irish Motor Neurone Disease Association.

But when the email dropped into my inbox saying that this play would be coming back to the stage, I was overcome with joy.

Since my diagnosis, I have had a burning desire to see this incredible production revived.

My involvement in the Marriage Equality referendum – and the subsequent book and play that resulted – is one of my proudest achievements.

But the book and the play have been a team effort. My pal Kevin Rafter helped me with the book, and there are lots of people to thank for the play: Colin Murphy, who turned all my interviews for the book into this great play; Pat Moylan, who took on the challenge of producing it; Gerry Stembridge, who directed; and all the great cast of actors which made it such a success.

I also have a sad memory: the barrister Noel Whelan, who played a key role in the referendum and who encouraged me to go out and travel around Ireland and record the stories for the book and play, has since passed away.

But I am so happy in Noel's memory that the play is coming back to the stage.

Finally, I want to use the words of the great Colm Tóibín about the book and the play:

'These stories collected by Charlie Bird, filled with bracing honesty and heart-breaking personal revelation, make clear that being gay in Ireland was perhaps a more essential aspect of Irish history and Irish reality than anyone was aware.'

From a dark place in my life, I have been lifted by the prospect of watching this great play on the stage again. So to every one of you who is making this possible, thank you from the bottom of my heart. And thank you for the LGBT+ community for extending the hand of friendship to me.

Charlie Bird
October 2022

# A note from the Pavilion Theatre

When I first met Charlie Bird prior to the 2019 performance of *A Day in May* at Pavilion Theatre, I was blown away by his passion, his enthusiasm and his commitment to this show – a show which resulted from his characteristically brilliant journalism in the aftermath of the Marriage Equality referendum. Going over and above what was expected, he pledged his unwavering support to help make that production a success. And a success it was, thanks in no small part to Charlie.

Watching RTÉ's *Charlie Bird: Loud and Clear* documentary this past June, I found myself deeply moved by this man whose work has informed and inspired so many and reflecting back on that first meeting three years prior and the subsequent discussions we'd had about a potential project. I texted writer Colin Murphy, asking if he felt the time might be right to revive *A Day in May*. He replied immediately to say that not only had he been thinking the same, but that Charlie had come to see the play as a big part of his life's work and legacy. That was all I needed to know.

After a turbulent period for the arts and Charlie's own saddening diagnosis, one positive contribution we as a venue felt we could make was to put this joyful, uplifting production back in front of audiences. Colin Murphy, the master playwright behind this adaptation, and peerless producer Pat Moylan have been indispensable at every stage in this process. Along with the help of the Department of Tourism, Culture, Arts, Gaeltacht, Sport and Media, Gerard Stembridge, Vincent Brightling, Sinead O'Doherty and Gerry Lundberg and the entire creative team, our charity partners and, of course, Charlie himself, I am delighted to see this revival of *A Day in May* become a reality.

We hope audiences will experience for themselves the restorative power of this play on our stage and give generously to Pieta and the Irish Motor Neurone Disease Association – charities very close to Charlie's heart – to support the essential work that they do. Now, more than ever, we need to celebrate those moments and people in our history that have brought us together to make the world a brighter place

Hugh Murray
Director, Pavilion Theatre
October 2022

## Pat Moylan – Producer

Pat Moylan's West End producing credits include the Olivier Award-winning *Stones in His Pockets* by Marie Jones (which also played on Broadway), *Alone it Stands* by John Breen, *The Shawshank Redemption* by Owen O'Neill and Dave Johns, *Thoroughly Modern Millie*, *Triple Espresso* and *Women on the Verge of HRT*. Her partners in these ventures were producers Paul Elliott, Duncan Weldon, Adam Kenwright, Breda Cashe, Donal Shiels and Jenny King.

In 2017 she produced *Angela's Ashes: The Musical* at the Bord Gais Theatre Dublin, Lime Tree Theatre Limerick and the Grand Opera House in Belfast. She was Artistic Director of Andrews Lane Theatre for eighteen years. In 2008 she was thrilled to have been nominated for a Special Award by *The Irish Times* for her work during that period. Pat formed Lane Productions in Dublin in 2001 with Breda Cashe and the successful duo produced a number of highly acclaimed shows including *Twelve Angry Men*, *Deadline*, *84 Charing Cross Road*, *I, Keano* and later they were joined by Donal Sheils and together they produced *The Field* with Brian Dennehy, *Haunted* by Edna O'Brien and *The Shawshank Redemption*.

Other credits include *The Secrets of Primrose Square* by Claudia Carroll (based on her own hugely successful novel); *Brighton Beach Memoirs* with Carole King; the highly acclaimed and award-winning *Beowulf: The Blockbuster*, written by and starring Bryan Burroughs, the show that completed an enormously successful engagement at the Irish Arts Center, New York, and was the number one show at the 2014 Edinburgh Fringe before playing at both the Adelaide and Perth Festivals; and *Tom Crean – Antarctic Explorer*, winner of a Fringe First in Edinburgh and then playing the Olympia Theatre Dublin. The production continues to tour. Also *A Galway Girl*, which played in Bewley's Theatre, Dublin, and at the Galway Arts Festival. In 2016 she again joined forces with Breda Cashe to produce the Irish premiere of *Driving Miss Daisy*.

With John McColgan and Moya Doherty she produced *A Tribute to Edna O'Brien* at the Gaiety Theatre in 2016. In addition to her theatre producing, film credits include the multi award winning short *The Breakfast* and the feature film *Borstal Boy*, directed by Peter Sheridan, starring Shawn Hatosy and Danny Dyer.

In 2014 Pat completed a five-year term as Chairman of the Arts Council of Ireland. She is currently on the Board of The Dublin Theatre Festival and is Chair of Music Network.

## Colin Murphy

Colin Murphy is a playwright, screenwriter and journalist. His first play, *Guaranteed!*, on the Irish bank guarantee of 2008, was acclaimed as 'a national event' by *The Irish Times* and nominated for an Irish Times Theatre Award. Plays since include *Bailed Out!*, on the Irish bailout, *Inside the GPO*, on the Easter Rising, *Haughey/Gregory* and *The Treaty*, all produced by Fishamble: The New Play Company. Short plays include *Make America Great Again* as part of *Home Theatre (Ireland)* at Draíocht and *The Voice of Michael Feery* as part of *14 Voices From The Bloodied Field* at the Abbey Theatre. Screen credits include: *The Guarantee*, nominated for an Irish Film and Television Academy Award, and *The Bailout*, both adapted from his plays and produced by John Kelleher Media; *State of Flux*, a docudrama on the 1921 Treaty debates, produced by Loosehorse; and the short films *Bonfire* (Fine Point Films) and *Leave to Remain* (Treasure Entertainment). Radio plays for RTÉ Drama on One include *Hamlet, Prince of Derry* and *The United States Versus Ulysses*. He writes a weekly column for the *Sunday Independent*.

# Charlie Bird

Charlie Bird is one of Ireland's most well-known journalists and has had a long and distinguished career in Irish public service broadcasting. In 1974 he joined RTÉ as a current affairs researcher. In 1980 he joined the newsroom as a reported. In a career which spanned almost four decades he held a number of positions: Chief News Reporter, Special Correspondent, Chief News Correspondent and Washington Correspondent. Over those years he was involved in many foreign assignments including the two Gulf Wars, the attacks on the Twin Towers and its aftermath. He also reported extensively on humanitarian stories around the world including the genocide in Rwanda, the Boxing Day tsunami and the earthquake in Haiti. Charlie also covered the troubles in Northern Ireland and the peace process. For over ten years he was RTÉ's designated link to the IRA.

He presented a number of major television documentaries travelling to both the North and the South Pole and dealing with issues of climate change. In November 2004 he was awarded an honorary Doctorate of Law by University College Dublin for his outstanding services to Irish journalism. In April 2015, he chaired the launch of the historic 'Yes Equality' marriage campaign.

Inspired by the extraordinary campaign, Charlie travelled the length and breadth of Ireland to meet some of the people most deeply affected by the referendum results. Their stories brought to life the reality of living in the shadow of inequality and oppression. The book and play, *A Day in May*, is a poignant record of their lives – of the pain, terror, confusion, the love and the laughter so beautifully captured by Charlie, amplifying the life-affirming impact of that day in May 2015 when Ireland said 'Yes' to marriage equality. In his foreword to the book *A Day in May*, the author Colm Toibin wrote, 'these stories collected by Charlie Bird, filled with bracing honesty and heart-breaking personal revelation, make clear that being gay in Ireland was perhaps a more essential aspect of Irish history and Irish reality than anyone was aware'.

Charlie has just been awarded the freedom of Co. Wicklow, a distinction he shares with only two other people: Daniel Day Lewis and Katie Taylor.

## Gerard Stembridge

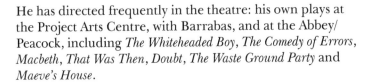

Gerard Stembridge was born in Limerick and educated at CBS Sexton Street and UCD.

He has worked in TV, film and radio as well as theatre. He has written eleven theatre plays including *Love Child*, *The Gay Detective* and *That Was Then*.

He has directed frequently in the theatre: his own plays at the Project Arts Centre, with Barrabas, and at the Abbey/ Peacock, including *The Whiteheaded Boy*, *The Comedy of Errors*, *Macbeth*, *That Was Then*, *Doubt*, *The Waste Ground Party* and *Maeve's House*.

He has published five novels.

Pat Moylan Productions and Pavilion Theatre
in association with A Day in May Trust Present

By Colin Murphy

Based upon the Original Book by Charlie Bird

Director         Gerard Stembridge
Lighting         Conleth White
Set and Costumes         Kate Moylan

Cast
(in alphabetical order)

Orla Fitzgerald
Conor Gormally
Anthony Kinahan
Mary Murray
Marion O'Dwyer
Mark O'Regan
Arthur Riordan
Sarah-Jane Scott

Producer         Pat Moylan
Associate Producer         Vincent Brightling
Publicity         O'Doherty Communications
Production Manager and
Stage Director         Miriam Duffy
Additional Audio Editing         Simon Kenny

Costume Assistant           Rebekkah Bustos
Finance and Accounts
Manager                   Linda Hyland

### For Pavilion Theatre

Director                  Hugh Murray
Marketing and Communications
Manager                   Dónal Kennedy
Operations Manager      Niall Gomes O'Connell
Technical Manager       Ronan Fingleton
Finance and Administration
Manager                   Paula Gray

The producers would like to thank: Claire Bird, Martin O'Brien, who helped get the initial funding, the INTO and the ASTI for their financial support for the 'A Day In May' project. Dublin Pride, Karl Hayden, Ruth Hegarty, Jasmine Daines Pilgrem, Holly ní Chiardha; Jim Culleton and all at Fishamble, Phillip MacMahon. Very special thanks to Eddie McGuinness, Jed Dowling and John McColgan.

An Roinn Turasóireachta, Cultúir, Ealaíon, Gaeltachta, Spóirt agus Meán
Department of Tourism, Culture, Arts, Gaeltacht, Sport and Media

PAT MOYLAN PRODUCTIONS    PAVILION THEATRE

pieta

Irish Motor Neurone Disease Association

LGBT IRELAND

## Vincent Brightling – Associate Producer

Vincent has been Assistant Producer to Pat Moylan since 2013. In that time he has worked with Pat on *The Secrets of Primrose Square* (Claudia Carroll), *Angela's Ashes – The Musical* (Adam Howell and Paul Hurt), *Beowulf: The Blockbuster* (Bryan Burroughs and David Horan), *The Field* (John B. Keane), *A Galway Girl* (Geraldine Aron), *Driving Miss Daisy* (Alfred Uhry), *Wrong Turn at Lungfish* (Garry Marshall and Lowell Ganz), *Stones in His Pockets* (Marie Jones) and *Tom Crean – Antarctic Explorer* (Aidan Dooley). Vincent was Associate Producer for Rosebuds Theatre on their highly acclaimed productions of *S Y R I U S* and *Click 2 Subscribe*.

He has also worked alongside Peter Sheridan on *Meet the Quarefella* (Jim Sheridan and Peter Sheridan), for Tall Tales on *Catastrophe* (Samuel Beckett) and The Read Co. on *Romantic Friction* (Michelle Read).

With Naoise Nunn he co-developed the late-night cabaret *Club Absinthe*.

# The Cast
## Orla Fitzgerald

Orla is a highly experienced Irish stage actress who has worked extensively in productions both in Ireland and the UK. She is recently played the role of Maureen in Martin McDonagh's *The Beauty Queen of Leenane*, a co-production between the Chichester Festival Theatre and the Lyric Hammersmith. She recently completed filming on ITV series *The Long Shadow*.

She recently appeared on our screens in the second and third series of BBC 3 series *The Young Offenders*.

Further theatre credits include the roles of Josephine in Stacey Gregg's *Josephine K and the Algorithms* at the Abbey Theatre, directed by Caitriona McLaughlin; Valerie in Conor McPherson's *The Weir*, directed by Rachel O'Riordan at the Sherman Theatre; Winnie Carney in *Inside the GPO* directed by Jim Culleton for Fishamble and performed inside Dublin's GPO; Abigail Colgan alongside Lorcan Cranitch and Peter Coonan in Ross Dungan's *Before Monsters Were Made*, directed by Ben Kidd for 15th Oak Productions; Clare in *Digging for Fire* directed by Matt Torney for Rough Magic Theatre Company (for which she received a Best Actress nomination in the Irish Times Theatre Awards) both at the Project Arts Centre; *Playboy of the Western World*, directed by Conall Morrison, and *Uncle Vanya*, directed by Mick Gordon, both at the Lyric Belfast.

Notable film work includes the role of Kate Walsh in *The Guarantee,* directed by Ian Power, and the role of Sinéad in Ken Loach's *The Wind that Shakes the Barley*, for which she was nominated for Best Actress and Best Breakthrough Artist at the Irish Film and Television Awards.

Further television credits include *Taken Down* for RTÉ; *The C Word* and *Holby Blue* for the BBC; the ITV series *Law and Order UK; The Last Furlong, Love is the Drug* and *Pure Mule: The Last Weekend* for RTÉ, and the E4 comedy *Cardinal Burns*

## Conor Gormally

Conor is a Belfast born and London based actor and writer. He is a graduate of the Oxford School of Drama.

Theatre credits include: *Our Generation* by Alecky Blythe (The National Theatre / Chichester Festival Theatre); the UK and Ireland tour of *Angela's Ashes the Musical* (Pat Moylan Productions); *A Day in May* (The Olympia Theatre); *The Ferryman* directed by Sam Mendes (The Gielgud Theatre, West End); *Affection* (Outbox Theatre); *World Mad* (Soho Theatre).

Short film: *Lúbtha* and *The Good Delusion*.

Voiceover: *Below* (Audible); *Luna Abyss* (Bonsai Collective).

## Anthony Kinahan

Born in Co Louth, Ireland, Anthony is a graduate of the Royal Central School of Speech and Drama, London.

Anthony has been fortunate enough to have gained some notable credits over the last few years – such as: *Conversations with Friends* (Dir: Lenny Abrahamson; Element Pictures); *Harry Wild* (Dir: Rob Burke; Acorn TV); *KIN* (Dir: Diarmuid Goggins/Tessa Hoffe; Bron Studios); *Locked In* (Dir: Leah Rossiter; Screen Ireland/Bow St – premiered at Galway Film Fleadh 2021); *A Day in May* (directed by Gerry Stembridge;

written by Colin Murphy, based on the book by Charlie Bird); Big Telly's *Right Up Your Street* with An Táin Theatre; *Red Rock*; *Vikings*; Rough Magic SEEDS *Assassins*; *Catch Chocolate*; and recurring character presenter Seánín Milseán in *The Beo Show* for RTEjr.

Anthony was Artist-in-Association at Droichead Arts Centre, Drogheda, for 2021 and also a recipient of an Arts Council Agility Award in the same period.

During this association, Anthony wrote and developed a one-man show, *Unguarded*. *Unguarded* will premiere at Droichead Arts Centre in October 2022 and will transfer to An Táin Arts Centre, Dundalk in February 2023.

Anthony is a performer/producer with Quintessence Theatre (Theatre Company-in-Residence of Droichead Arts Centre, Drogheda, 2019–20 and Theatre Company-in-Residence of An Táin Arts Centre, Dundalk, 2015–19). In autumn 2016, Anthony co-created and appeared in *Cracks* with Quintessence Theatre (in association with An Táin Art Centre). Quintessence took their acclaimed comedy *The Star of Chester's Lane* on a National Tour in Winter 2021.

Anthony also recently appeared as the Matt in Quintessence Theatre's play *Behind Locked Doors* as part of the Drogheda Arts Festival 2022 (and later transferred to An Táin Arts Centre, Dundalk).

Some of Anthony's other notable credits with Quintessence include: *The Curious Case of Albert Cashier* (due to tour in 2022); *#Me Too, Three, Four*; *Boy, Girl, Repeat*; *Warrior of the Táin; Dracula* ... among others.

Anthony is also the founder and Artistic Director of Act Out Youth Theatre in Meath.

## Mary Murray

Mary's theatre credits include: *Outrage*, *Stronger*, *Embargo*, *Tiny Plays 24/7*, *Tiny Plays for Ireland and America* (Washington and New York tour), *Tiny Plays for Ireland 1 & 2*, *Noah and The Tower Flower* (revival tours to New York, Romania and Bulgaria), *End Of The Road*, *The Pride Of Parnell Street* (Winner Of Best Actress 2009 at The First Irish Theatre Festival in New York and also Best Actress at the MAMCA awards 2008) and *Turning Point* (Fishamble Theatre Company), *Ulysses* (Tron Theatre tours in China, Britain and Ireland), *Christmas Craicers*, *Kissing the Witch*, *No Smoke Without Fire*, *Close to the Sun* and *Bug* (Corps Ensemble), *Holy Mary* (Breda Cashe Productions), *A Day in May* (Pat Moylan Productions), *Wild Sky* (T42 Productions -Ireland and New York tour), *No Smoke Without Fire* and *Chancers* (Viking Theatre), *Arrah Na Pogue* (Abbey Theatre), *Boss Grady's Boys* (Gaiety), *Bogboy* (Tall Tales), *Twelve Days in May* (Liberty Hall Theatre), *Macbecks* (Long Road Productions), *Off Plan*, *Splendour* (RAW Theatre Company), *Sleeping Beauty* and *Miss Julie* (Landmark Productions), *The Alice Trilogy* (The Abbey Theatre – Winner of Best Supporting Actress at The Irish Times Theatre Awards), *Macbeth* (Second Age), *Operation Easter* and *Five Kinds Of Silence* (Calypso Productions), *Family Stories* (B*spoke Theatre Company – Irish Times Best Supporting Actress Award Nominee 2005), *Oh When The Hoops* (Liberty Productions), *Playing Politics* (Dublin Theatre Festival), *Knocknashee* (Tall Tales), *The Grapes Of Wrath* (Storytellers Theatre Company) and *On Raftery's Hill* (Druid/Royal Court-International Tour.

Her film and television credits include: *The Wonder*, *Valhalla*, *The Long Weekend*, *Benedict's Feast*, *Let The Wrong One In*, *Dead Still*, *Don't Talk to Strangers*, *The Letters*, *Please Like Me*, *Each Other*, *The Wedding Ring*, *134*, *Bridget and Eamon*, *Rising/*

*Falling*, *The Emerald Stone*, *Grace*, *Fingerprints*, *Hot Knives*, *Rising/Falling*, *Love/Hate* seasons 3, 4 and 5 (nominated best leading and supporting actress in television at the Irish Film and Television Awards), *Poison Pen*, *Penny Dreadful*, *Stalker*, *My Whole Half Life*, *City Of Hate*, *The Red Line*, *Death Of A Superhero*, *Angel*, *Two Hearts*, *Situations Vacant*, *The Con Saw Tina Effect*, *Eamon*, *El Juego Del Ahorcado*, *Little White Lie*, *Blue Soup*, *Prosperity*, *Frankie*, *Bitterness*, *What If?*, *King of Nothing*, *Adam And Paul*, *W.C.*, *The Magdalene Sisters*, *On The Edge*, *Accelerator*, *Crushproof*, *A Great Party*, *Recoil*, *The Marriage Of Strongbow and Aoife*, *The Very Stuff*, *ER* (T na G), *Fair City*, *Love Is The Drug*, *The Big Bow Wow*, *Ambassador* and *Random Passage*.

Her voice-over work includes: Animations – *Little Allan*, *Rabbit Academy*, *My Toothfairy Troublemaker*, *Captain Sabertooth*, *Royals Next Door*, *Two by Two Overboard*, *Casparade*, *Louis n Luca*, *Louis And His Friends From Outerspace*, *Niko 2*, *Thor – The Edda Chronicles*. Documentaries – *Paying For Sex* (RTE-Reality Bites), *1916 – An Irish Rebellion*. Radio Plays – *The Pride of Parnell Street* (BBC3), *Two Thieves*, *Secrets*, *Paid in Full*, *Captives*, *Going Straight* (Newstalk), *Offerings*, *Lennon's Guitar*, *The Sorting Office Of The Universe*, *Bog Boy*, *Appearances*, *Moving Day* and *Happy Hour* (RTE), *Baby Be Mine* (BBC Radio 4), *The Lost Patriot* (Tinpot Productions). Other – she narrated *Can Lilly O' Shea Come Out To Play* for The Book On One and excerpts of *Tenement Life* for The Dublin History Museum.

Mary is the director of Visions Drama School and Agency: www.visionsdrama.com

## Marion O'Dwyer

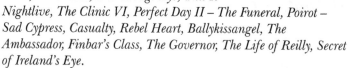

Film includes *God's Creatures, The Silence of Mercy, Fanacht, Finding You, End of Sentence, Robot Ben, Love, Rosie, Covet, Suzie Cohen's Holy Communion, An Old Fashioned Christmas, Ondine, Agnes Brown, Green.*

Television includes *Miss Scarlet and the Duke, A Dangerous Fortune, Romantic Road, Love Hate, The Savage Eye, This Is Nightlive, The Clinic VI, Perfect Day II – The Funeral, Poirot – Sad Cypress, Casualty, Rebel Heart, Ballykissangel, The Ambassador, Finbar's Class, The Governor, The Life of Reilly, Secret of Ireland's Eye.*

Theatre includes: for the Abbey and Peacock: *Drama at Inish, The Unmanageable Sisters, By the Bog of Cats, The Government Inspector, Bookworms, The Rivals, Big Love, The Crucible, School for Scandal, Drama at Inish, The Plough and the Stars, That Was When, The Memory of Water, Portia Coughlan* (also Royal Court), *Kevin's Bed, The Only True History of Lizzy Flynn, Dancing at Lughnasa* (also Sydney Opera House), *Moving, The Silver Tassie, You Can't Take It With You, Wonderful Tennessee* (also Plymouth Theatre, Broadway).

For the Gate Theatre: *The Red Shoes, The Heiress, The Importance of Being Earnest, Pride and Prejudice, A Streetcar Named Desire, A Woman of No Importance, The Speckled People, Cat on a Hot Tin Roof, The Deep Blue Sea, Stella by Starlight, A Tale of Two Cities, Pride and Prejudice, The Threepenny Opera, Our Country's Good, An Ideal Husband, Twelfth Night, Fathers and Sons.*

For Druid Theatre Company: *Be Infants in Evil, The Silver Tassie, The Loves of Cass Maguire, Poor Beast in the Rain, Lovers Meeting, The Donahue Sisters.*

Further theatre work: *The Mai* (Decadent Theatre Co), *Philadelphia Here I Come!* (Lyric Theatre Belfast), *The*

*Cavalcaders* (Decadent Theatre Co), *Payback!* (Bewleys and tour), *Philadelphia Here I Come!* (Gaiety Theatre), *Mrs Whippy* (City Theatre), *Sky Road* (Theatre Royal Waterford), *Roberto Zucco* (Bedrock, *Casanova's Limp* (Bewley's Café Theatre), *Shadow of a Gunman* and *Sive* (Tricycle Theatre), *The Vagina Monologues* (Gaiety Theatre), *Molly Sweeney* (Bristol Old Vic), *From Both Hips* (Tivoli and Glasgow Tron), *Juno and the Paycock* (Gaiety Theatre and Chicago Theatre Festival)

## Mark O'Regan

Mark has recently worked on *Sisters*, a new comedy drama series, and he worked on the feature film In *The Land of Saints and Sinners* opposite Liam Neeson, due for release 2023.

Mark appeared in season one and two of *Blood* opposite Adrian Dunbar on Virgin Media One.

Recent theatre credits include: Mark recently appeared in the World Premiere of *Circle of Friends* at The Gaiety Theatre. He appeared in *Philadelphia Here I Come* at the Cork Opera House. He appeared on stage in the Abbey's production of *Drama at Inish*.

Mark's work at The Gaiety includes *Borstal Boy*, *Translations*, *Moll*, *Taking Steps*, *Aladdin*, *The Field*, and recently *The Chastitute*. Mark most recently appeared in *Assassins* at the Gate Theatre and *Angela's Ashes The Musical* at the Bord Gais Theatre.

Film and television credits include: *Nighthawks*, *Revenge*, *Upwardly Mobile*, *Showbands* (RTE); *Father Ted* (Channel 4); *Anytime Now* (BBC); *The Dawning*, *The Commitments*, *The Life of Reilly*, *Black Day at Blackrock*, *Angela's Ashes*, *Anytime Now*, *Into the West*, *Uncle Bill's Barrell*, *The Last of the High Kings*, *Leap Year*, *Milo* and, more recently, *Wait for Me*, due for release later this year.

At the Gate Theatre he has appeared in *Assassins*, *Juno and the Paycock*, *A Month in the Country*, *Pride and Prejudice*, *The Vortex*, *Arcadia*, *The Old Curiosity Shop*, *Sweeney Todd*, *Festen*, *Fathers and Sons*, *Sharon's Grave*, *Peer Gynt*, *Three Sisters*, *The Threepenny Opera*, *Twelfth Night*, *London Assurance*, *A Christmas Carol*, *As You Like It*, *All My Sons* and *The Rivals*.

His work at the Abbey Theatre includes *Alice in Funderland*, *The School for Scandal*, *I Do Not Like Thee Dr Fell*, *The Plough and the Stars*, *Juno and the Paycock*, *The Memory of Water*, *The Invisible Mending Company*, *Observe the Sons of Ulster Marching Towards the Somme*, *Saint Joan*, *The Last Apache Reunion*, *A Strange Occurrence on Ireland's Eye*, *Chamber Music* and *The Broken Jug*.

Other work: *King Ubu* (Galway Arts Festival); *Bleeding Poets* (New Theatre); *The Ghost* Show (West Cork Fit-Up Festival); *Eejit of Love* (Samuel Beckett Theatre); *Dodgems* (O'Reilly Theatre); *Anglo the Musical* (Bord Gais Theatre); *Spenser's Laye* (Assembly Rooms, Edinburgh); *Twelfth Night* (Japan); *Moll* (Manhattan Town Hall, New York); *The Cripple of Inishmaan* (Centaur Theatre, Montreal); *Woman and Scarecrow* (National tour and Centre Culturel Irlandais, Paris) and *Pride and Prejudice* at the Hong Kong Arts Festival.

## Arthur Riordan

Arthur Riordan is an actor and writer, and a founder member of Rough Magic Theatre Company, with whom he has appeared in many productions, including *Peer Gynt*, *A Solemn Mass For A Full Moon In Summer*, *Improbable Frequency*, and, most recently, *The Tempest*.

Other recent performances include *Philadelphia Here I Come* (Cork Opera House); *King Lear* (Play in a Van); *The Alternative* (Fishamble, the New Play Company); *From Under The Bed* (Big Guerilla Productions); *Krapp's Last Tape*

(Theatre Royal, Waterford); *Kings Of The Kilburn High Road* (Gaiety Theatre); *Swing* (Fishamble).

He has also performed with Druid, The Abbey and Peacock, Pan Pan, The Passion Machine, and many more.

Arthur has also made numerous TV and film appearances including *Debutante*, *Holy Island*, *A Sunken Place*, *Lucky In Love*, *Out Of Here*, *Refuge*, *Borstal Boy*, *Ripper Street*, *Pitch 'N' Putt with Joyce and Beckett*, and others.

Arthur's plays include an adaptation of Joyce's *A Portrait Of The Artist As A Young Man*; *The Train* (music by Bill Whelan); *Improbable Frequency* (music by Bell Helicopter); an adaptation of *Peer Gynt* (music by Tarab); the libretto for Andrew Synnott's *Dubliners* opera (Opera Theatre Company/ Wexford Festival Opera); an adaptation of Flann O'Brien's *Slattery's Sago Saga* (Performance Corporation); *Rap Eire* (Bickerstaffe) and *Shooting Gallery* (Bedrock Productions) – these last two co-written with Des Bishop.

## Sarah-Jane Scott

Film and TV: *Dead Happy* (Playground Pictures); *Rose Plays Julie* (Samson Films); *The Opening* (Piju Films); *The Marijuana Method* (Wildseed Studios); *Stay* (Samson Films); *Art Is...* (New Troy Productions).

Theatre: *Appropriate* (1st Irish Festival NYC/ Guna Nua); *Mirrors* (International Literature Festival Dublin); *Brilliant* (Fevered Sleep – Beijing – Arts Space for Kids); *100 Great Plays for Women* (National Theatre); *Sonnet Walks* (Shakespeare's Globe); *The Planet and Stuff* (Polka Theatre/Tonic Theatre Polka Theatre/Tonic Theatre); *May Contain Nuts* (Nabokov: Present Tense); *What's in My Box* (Bush Theatre); *Alice and Victor* (BlockSEVENTEEN); *Radio Silence*, *I Bet You* and *What About the Rent?* (The Bell Collective); *The Comedy of Errors* (Word of Mouth Productions); *And the Act Going Home Tonight Is…, Dryfight* and *Game Girl, Game Boy* (DryWrite); *The Seagull* (Bottled Spider Productions); *Five Twosomes* (The Rose Theatre Studio); *Blood Wedding* (Oxford School of Drama); *A Midsummer Night's Dream* (Blenheim Palace).

Winner: Lustrum Award for Excellence

Winner: Bairbre Dowling Spirit of the Festival Award

## Conleth White

His work encompasses a broad range of fields from theatre, live art, dance, opera and site specific.

Site specific work includes *The Tempest* (Kilmainham Gaol); *Binlids*, for DubbelJoint in Whiterock, Belfast and Angel Orenzans Centre, New York; the Field Day/Tinderbox co-production of Stewart Parker's *Northern Star* in the First Presbyterian Church, Belfast Festival. For Kabosh: *This Is What We Sang* in the Belfast Synagogue; *1 in 5* in the Roe Valley Hospital (former workhouse), Limavady; *Belfast By Moonlight* in St George's Church, Belfast. In 14 Henrietta St, Dublin, for The International Literature Festival 2015: *The Only Jealousy of Emer*.

Other diverse work has included imagery/light for *Translations*, directed by Adrian Dunbar, in the Millennium Forum, Derry, and the Kings, Edinburgh; imagery/light for *Tejas Verdes & POENA 5X1* (Inside-Intelligence, Edinburgh Festival 2013/16); set/light/imagery for the 36th (Ulster) Division Memorial committee presentation of *From The Shipyard to the Somme* in East Belfast (2013). He toured lighting to swimming-pools in Belgrade, Taiwan, Denmark and the UK with Big Telly's productions of *The Little Mermaid* (2005/6). In 2017, he created imagery for Kabosh's dramatic reading of *North* by Seamus Heaney in the Seamus Heaney Home Place, and imagery and light for *A Queer Ceili* at the Marty Forsythe (in the Marty Forsythe, West Belfast 2019); he also created lighting for *Floating World's Elders Forest Project* in the Killruddery Estate 2022.

For Partisan Productions (Belfast): set/light/imagery for *100 Years On*, a trilogy of short plays (2013/4); *The Prettiest Thing*, in the Brook Centre, Twinbrook (2014); *East Belfast Boy*, Ballymac Centre, and *The Colin Nativity Dairy Farm* (2015); *East Belfast Girl*, Ballymac Centre (2016); *A Tried And Tested Account* in the Engine Room, Portview Trade Centre and East Belfast; *Granny* in the Ballymac Centre (2018); *Time Of Your Life* in Ballymac Centre and tour (2019).

Other theatre work has included set, costume, imagery and light for *Entitled,* written and directed by Fionnuala Kennedy of Macha (The Mac 2017); *Terra Nova's Belfast Tempest* in T13; light/imagery for *F.A.T.D.A.D.* (Complex 2017) and *Dublin Will Show You How* (Complex/Abbey 2019); lighting for *Love in the Wild* by Lisa Walsh, directed by Peter Sheridan in Axis-Ballymun (2018). For Kabosh: lighting for *Before You Go* and *The Shedding of Our Skin* (streaming 2021 and live 2022) and *Callings* in 2022.

From 2012 to 2019, Conleth has been involved in the Moving Bodies Festival of Live Art and Butoh in Dublin and Turin.

*A Day in May* was first presented at the Olympia Theatre, Dublin, by A Day in May Trust in association with Pat Moylan & MCD Productions, on 24 June 2018 – the twenty-fifth anniversary of the decriminalisation of homosexuality – with the following cast:

Amy Conroy
Conor Gormally
Anthony Kinahan
Clodagh Mooney Duggan
Mary Murray
Helen Norton
Mark O'Regan
Arthur Riordan

*Director*   Gerard Stembridge
*Lighting*   Conleth White
*Set and Costume*   Kate Moylan

# A Day in May

## Characters

**William** ⎫ *Members of the Gay and Lesbian*
**John** ⎭ *Equality Network (GLEN)*
**Siobhán** ⎫
**Mary** ⎭ *Members of the campaign group Marriage Equality*
**Victor**, *seventies, from Mayo*
**Nora**, *thirties or forties, from Athlone*
**Seán**, *twenties or early thirties, from the Midlands*
**Jane**, *forties, from Cork*
**Gill**, *twenties or thirties, from Roscommon*
**Julie**, *twenties or early thirties, a Dub*
**Fr Joe**, *a native Irish speaker*
**Katherine**, *fifties or older, from West Cork*
**Gareth**, *early twenties*
**Síofra**, *twenties, from Longford*

*Other characters as occur throughout the script*

## Staging

*In the original production, an ensemble of four women and four men played all the parts, with all remaining on stage throughout. The set and props consisted simply of eight chairs, two costume rails, a sparkling backdrop and a glitter ball. As actors stepped forward, out of the ensemble, to assume the characters for the individual stories, other members of the ensemble would hand them any costume or prop items they needed.*

*Play the joy and humour of the story and the sadness will take care of itself.*

**Victor's Story**

**Victor** *steps forward and addresses the audience. He is in his seventies.*

**Victor**   There was a young fella one time in the snooker club, in Ballina, Paddy. And we were going up the stairs into the club. And Paddy put his hand over –

(*Gesturing to his hand.*) Just there, on me . . . I thought that was odd, but, eh, I didn't – I didn't dislike it. I felt good from it, to be honest with you . . . So Paddy and myself met a few times. But we never had any – What would you call it? Jesus, I don't know – I think we had – maybe masturbating a bit – But there was nothing else . . . no 'penetration' . . . I never had sex . . . I have never had any penetration sex at all.

I was living in a flat, at that time. And there was a fella called Gerry living next door, with his wife and kids. And Gerry and I were coming in from the pub one Sunday night, and Paddy was waiting for me in the archway at the entrance to the building. And Gerry said –

**Gerry** (*to* **Victor**)   Who is that bastard down there?

**Victor** (*to* **Gerry**)   I don't know.

**Gerry** (*rolling up his sleeves*)   That bastard's a queer.

**Victor** (*to audience*)   There was a little coal shed down at the bottom of the building. And Gerry got Paddy in there and he said to me –

**Gerry** (*to* **Victor**)   You stand there, and don't let him out the door.

**Victor**   I never had anything to do with Paddy after that . . . That was . . . That was a long time ago.

**1983–1993**

*'It Ain't Necessarily So' by Bronski Beat plays. A disco. General dancing at first, and then eyes meet across the dance floor and the dancers couple up. The male couple are left alone on stage, and then this moment of intimacy is suddenly transformed into a moment of violence as the 'queerbashing' occurs.*

**Newsreader**    Five Dublin youths, who killed thirty-one-year-old Declan Flynn when they went what they described as 'queer bashing' in Fairview Park, have walked free from the Central Criminal Court. The jury found them guilty of manslaughter, but Mr Justice Seán Gannon imposed suspended sentences, saying –

**Judge Seán Gannon**    There is no element of *correction* that is required. All of these young men come from good homes and experienced care and affection.

**Chorus**    March, 1983. Days to go: 11,762.

**Activist One**    We can't just sit back and take this.

**Activist Two**    What the fuck can we do about it?

**Activist One**    A march.

**Activist Three** (*horrified*)    In public?

**Activist One**    Like those 'Pride' marches they've been having in the States.

**Activist Three**    Would we be photographed – in the papers?

**Activist One**    We could march to Fairview, in honour of Declan.

*The march happens, interrupted by the News.*

**Chorus**    April, 1983. Days to go: 11,717.

**Newsreader**    The law making homosexual acts a criminal offence has been upheld by the Supreme Court after it rejected the claim by the Trinity lecturer, Mr David Norris, that the law was unconstitutional. The majority judgement was delivered by the Chief Justice, Mr Justice O'Higgins.

**Chief Justice O'Higgins**   Homosexual conduct may lead a mildly homosexually-orientated person into a way of life from which he may never recover . . . An open and general increase in homosexual activity in any society must have serious consequences of a harmful nature so far as marriage is concerned.

**Activist Two**   Norris will have to challenge it.

**Activist Three**   That was the Supreme Court – the end of the road.

**Activist One**   Europe! He can sue the Government.

*The Government assembles at a Cabinet meeting.*

**Secretary General**   Ahem, Taoiseach?

**Taoiseach**   Yes, Secretary General –

**Secretary General**   The next item on the agenda is the Norris case at the European Court of Human Rights.

**Taoiseach**   Ah.

**Secretary General**   The Government has to decide whether it wishes to defend the State's current legal position outlawing homosexuality.

**Cabinet Minister**   Well clearly we have to defend our sovereignty. We can't have Europe meddling in our own unique perspective on moral issues.

**Taoiseach**   I wonder is there some wiggle room in the legislation – some ambiguity we could exploit . . . What is the *precise* offence in the Act?

**Secretary General**   The technical term used is 'the abominable act of buggery'.

**Taoiseach**   Ah.

(*Musing.*) Let's refer it to the Attorney General.

**Secretary General**   Yes, Taoiseach.

**Chorus**   October, 1988.

*She pauses, about to give the 'days to go', but gives up.*

**ECHR Crier** (*calling the court to attention*)    La Cour! La Cour européenne des Droits de l'Homme est maintenant en session.

**ECHR Judge**    La Cour dit, par huit voix contre six, qu'il y a violation de l'article huit de la Convention contre Monsieur David Norris.

**Activist Two**    Norris has won!

**Activist Three**    We're legal!

**Activist One**    Well, not quite – yet.

**Activist Three**    Why not?

**Activist One**    The government now has to bring in legislation to enforce the ruling.

**Activist Three**    How long will that take?

**Activist One**    It should be pretty straightforward . . . I'd say about . . .

(*A glance to the audience.*) Five years.

**Chorus**    June 24, 1993.

**Ceann Comhairle**    The Criminal Law (Sexual Offences) Bill, 1993: Second Stage. I call upon Deputy Paul McGrath, Fine Gael.

*As he speaks, the activists gather round him, putting on public exhibitions.*

**Paul McGrath TD**    It is not one's fault that one is attracted to somebody of the same sex – and it is wrong to encourage or condone attacks on gay people . . . But I am concerned about the possible effect on Irish society of this Bill. Will we now see exhibitions in *public* by homosexuals . . . holding hands, kissing, cuddling?

Ceann Comhairle, will we be faced with requests that homosexuals should be allowed to *marry*?

**William's Story**

*One of the Activists steps forward, now as* **William**. *He is in his late forties or fifties.*

**William**    I remember being seven and knowing that something was different. And I didn't know what that something was. I didn't have any name for it. But the thing I knew was that this had to be absolutely hidden . . . If they found out, it was obvious what would happen: I would have to leave school; I would lose my friends; I would lose my family . . .

It was a piece of myself that couldn't ever be said to anyone, anywhere . . . A gaping hole. I thought people would see the mark of me being different. I was afraid they would know if I met their eyes . . . So, I didn't meet anyone's eyes. I was terribly lonely, because I was going to be dishonest in every friendship I ever had, because I was never ever going to say this core thing that mattered . . .

I saw nothing about being gay, anywhere . . . I scoured the library to see was there anything . . . The only thing I ever found was in a book by a zoologist, Desmond Morris – *Manwatching: A Field Guide to Human Behaviour* . . .

The only *people* I knew of who were gay were David Norris, who was a Joycean scholar, and John Inman, from *Are You Being Served?* . . . and I wasn't either of those.

Eventually, when I came up to Dublin, I found Books Upstairs, which was in the George's Street Arcade. And it had the newspaper, *Gay Community News*. And on a Saturday, I would go in to town and I would walk up and down the Arcade for an hour to figure out was there anyone I knew anywhere around, and then I would go into the shop, and out, and I wouldn't even pick it up.

I was trying to find an image of myself . . . somewhere . . . anywhere . . . just something that said, there are others.

**Dáil Éireann – 2006**

**William** *and* **John** *shake hands with two Labour TDs.*

**Chorus**    February 2006. Dáil Éireann.

**Labour TD One**    There's likely to be a vote called – we may just have a few minutes.

**William**    I'll get straight to the point. Gay couples have the same love, the same commitment, as straight couples. They should have the same protections.

**Labour TD One**    *Legal* protections?

**William**    Marriage.

**Labour TD Two**    You won't get that past the Supreme Court.

**Labour TD One**    Gay marriage would need constitutional change.

**Labour TD Two**    Which would mean a referendum.

**Labour TD One**    And could you win a referendum?

*Beat.*

**William**    No.

**Labour TD One**    We're prepared to propose a civil unions bill.

**Labour TD Two**    Civil partnership.

**Labour TD One**    A stepping stone.

**William**    But we don't / want a stepping stone.

**Labour TD Two**    Concentrate on the *substantive* change – the rights that marriage brings. Itemise them. Tick them off, one by one.

**Labour TD One**    Marriage in all but name.

**John**    The name is important.

**Labour TD Two**    The name is what scares people.

**Labour TD One**    If we're to do this – we need you on board.

**John** (*to* **William**)    It'll be seen as a sell-out.

**Labour TD One**    GLEN is the voice of the gay community – you have to be vocal.

**Labour TD Two**    If we're going to stick our heads out on it, you have to back us.

**William**    We'll take heat for this.

**Labour TD One**    Welcome to politics.


**Nora's Story**

**Nora** *steps forward. She is in her thirties or forties, from Athlone.*

**Nora**    I came out when I was sixteen. But I didn't know I was 'coming out'. I didn't know . . . any of the language. All I knew is that myself and another sixteen-year-old girl, we were in love and it felt really good, and everything made sense to me then, and I was really happy, and I thought everyone would be as happy for me as I was, so I told them . . .

*Beat.*

Athlone was a very small town at the time.

*Beat.*

My girlfriend's mother went into where I worked –

**Girlfriend's Mother**    That girl is unnatural! You are to *fire* her!

**Nora**    And any time she saw me, she would scream –

**Girlfriend's Mother**    You filthy thing, stay away from my daughter!

**Nora**    One evening, I had been out for a walk, I was coming back, up the back of Strand Street. And something was thrown over my head. There was male and female voices – laughing – having the craic. I was on the ground. They were shouting

**Female Attacker**   Lezzy!

**Male Attacker**   Ye fuckin queer!

**Nora**   and all that. And kicking me . . . I went to the guards, because that's what you do.

*The **Garda** opens his station book to record the incident.*

**Garda**   Were they robbing you, or what?

**Nora**   No . . . It's because I have a girlfriend.

**Garda** (*closing his book*)   Well, love . . . What do you expect?

## 2006–2007

**Chorus**   December, 2006. Days to go: 3,081.

**Newsreader**   The High Court has found that a lesbian couple do not have the right to marry. Ms Justice Elizabeth Dunne found that, under the Constitution, marriage was confined to persons of the opposite sex.

**Judge Elizabeth Dunne**   Dr Ann Louise Gilligan and Dr Katherine Zappone referred frequently in the course of this case to the 'changing consensus' on same-sex marriage but I have to say, there is little evidence of that. There has been some *limited* support for it but, in truth, it is difficult to see that as a consensus, changing or otherwise.

**Siobhán**   The legal route's not going to work.

**Mary**   What's the alternative?

**Siobhán**   We're going to have to run a *political* campaign – for marriage equality.

**Chorus**   November, 2007. Days to go: 2,759.

**Newsreader**    The Minister for Justice has announced plans to legislate for civil partnerships. This has been welcomed by the Gay and Lesbian Equality Network, GLEN, but the gay rights group Marriage Equality has criticised the proposal.

**Siobhán** *and* **Mary** *prepare themselves.*

**Mary**    I don't know why you agreed to this.

**Siobhán**    GLEN want to work with us.

**Mary**    GLEN are a bunch of middle-class, middle-aged *men*. Think they speak for the rest of us. The fucking patriarchy.

**William** *and* **John** *have arrived, and overheard her.*

**William**    Hi.

*Awkward 'Hi's all round.*

**William**    We want to agree a common campaign on civil partnership.

**Siobhán**    Civil partnership is a distraction –

**Mary**    It's a humiliation –

**William**    It's far from perfect. But it's concrete progress.

**Siobhán**    It institutionalises a second-class citizenship.

**Mary**    How does that count as progress?

**William**    Don't let the perfect be the enemy of the good! It can be a stepping stone to marriage.

**Siobhán**    It could be the end of the road. We might never *get* marriage.

**William**    What's your alternative?

**Siobhán**    No stepping stones.

**Mary**    Go all out for marriage.

**William**    We won't get the political support.

**Mary**    So we *force* them!

**Siobhán**   We take the campaign onto the streets – to the gates of the Dáil.

**William**   We're trying to win over the people *inside* the Dáil – hurling abuse at them from the gates is not necessarily the best way to do that.

**John**   Civil partnership is marriage in all but name.

**Mary**   This is about more than a legal contract – it's about *ritual*.

**John**   What happened to the radical feminist critique of marriage? I thought you wanted to get *rid* of it as an institution –

**Mary**   Oh God that old stuff – it's so conservative and / predictable

**John**   'Conservative'? You're the ones that want to go shopping for wedding dresses.

**William**   If we split on this in public, the politicians might pull their support . . .

**Siobhán**   We can't back something our community is *against*.

**William**   If you're serious politically, you have to be prepared to take that hit.

**Mary**   Don't lecture us!

**Siobhán**   We can't support you on it.

**Mary**   It's a sell-out.

**Siobhán**   We're going to run a campaign for *marriage*.

**John**   You're playing politics with people's lives.

**Mary**   Sure what would we know about playing politics? I thought that game was just for the big boys.

**William**   Don't destroy what we're doing –

**Siobhán**   I can't promise anything.

**Seán's Story**

**Seán** *steps forward. He is in his twenties or early thirties, from the Midlands.*

**Seán**    I didn't speak in secondary school. I was also, like, really dyslexic. And I was taught really poorly. So I was still doing, like, 'a, b, c', and stuff that a five-year-old would be doing, when I was fifteen. So not only was I gay – I also felt fucking retarded . . .

**Kid One**    Fucking retard!

**Kids One & Two** (*sing-song*)    Seán the retard, Seán the retard . . .

**Seán**    But the worst thing you can be called in an all-boys school is –

**Kid Three** (*with loathing*)    *Faggot.*

**Kids** (*chorus, laughing*)    Faggot, faggot, faggot . . .

**Seán**    You know, 'diversity' was not celebrated in Ardee in 2003 – it was like, if you are not good at soccer and not good at academics, you are good at nothing. And I was good at nothing . . .

I was raised Catholic – it was really drilled into my head. So when I realised I was a faggot, I thought, 'I am going to hell anyway, so . . .' And so I found myself standing on my window ledge, two flights up, thinking . . . 'If I flip properly, I'll crack my neck' . . . I stood there for maybe two minutes . . . And then I remembered a guy that my dad worked with, who fell off a ladder. He cracked his neck. But it didn't kill him. He ended up paralysed for the rest of his life, eating through a straw. 'Fuck,' I thought. 'If I fuck *this* up, I won't even get another chance to kill myself.' And then I got into bed and cried.

When I turned eighteen, my sister bought me a bottle of vodka. And I came out to my mum. My mum is pretty cool. She doesn't have a problem with anyone.

**Seán's Mum** *screams.*

**Seán**   And when she calmed down, she just said –

**Seán's Mum**   It's a really lonely life, Seán.

**Seán**   There was a guy in our town when I was growing up
. . . Larry.

**Seán's Dad**   Don't be going near Larry now,
Seán –

**Seán's Mum** *(agreeing)*   He's –

**Seán**   He never married, never had any kids –

**Seán's Dad**   He's a bit, eh –

**Seán**   And everyone assumed he was –

**Seán's Mum** *(agreeing with his dad)*   Funny . . .

**Seán**   gay.

**Seán's Mum** *(awkward)*   Ah now –

**Seán's Dad** *(embarrassed)*   There's no need to –

**Seán**   And, back in the nineties, in rural Ireland, if you
were gay, people assumed you were a paedophile . . .

**Seán's Mum** *and* **Dad** *look even more uncomfortable.*

**Seán**   And so they stayed away from you.

**Seán's Mum**   Seán . . . Larry's dead . . . He was there for
three days before they found him. His meals-on-wheels had
piled up outside his door . . . That's how they knew
something was wrong.

**Seán**   That's what my mum was afraid of . . .

**Seán's Mum**   Why don't you just *try* dating girls, love?

**Seán**   She was afraid I would turn out like Larry.

**Seán's Mum**   God no –

**Seán**'s **Dad**    Ah now –

**Seán**    And my dad, he's a very devout man . . . a very GAA, soccer-playing, Irish dad. He was always annoyed that I was such a wimpy kid. So he tried to get me into football. And his way of doing that was plastering my room with . . . Chelsea posters . . . So I just developed a crush on Roberto di Matteo.

When I was twenty-one, I fell head over heels in love with a guy called Padraic. And I was, like, 'This cannot be wrong! This is something that I should –'

*He breaks off.*

**Seán** (*nervous*)    Dad –

**Seán**'s **Dad** (*preoccupied*)    Hmm?

**Seán** (*getting upset*)    Dad, I have something I . . . I need to tell you . . .

**Seán**'s **Dad**    Seán?

**Seán** (*very upset, shaking*)    Dad, like . . .

**Seán**'s **Dad** (*under his breath*)    Oh Jesus.

**Seán**    I am . . . gay, Dad.

**Seán**'s **Dad**    Oh thank Christ!

**Seán** (*confused*)    What?

**Seán**'s **Dad**    Of course you're gay. I always knew you were gay.

**Seán**    Of course –?

**Seán**'s **Dad**    I thought you were going to say you'd AIDS, or something.

**Seán**    You *always* –?

**Seán**'s **Dad**    I knew you were gay when you were seven, chasing other fellas in your Batman outfit.

**Seán**  You knew?

**Seán's Dad**  It's not a problem.

**Seán**  Well then why the fuck didn't you let me know that years ago?

(*To audience.*) So when I went to college, I said, Fuck it, I am a faggot – I don't give a shit who knows – I am going to introduce myself as gay. At the time you could tell if someone was gay by them having a man bag, or wearing a scarf indoors. Terrible stereotypes, but stereotypes are there for a reason. And it was really liberating, because then you meet loads of other gays, because they can spot you a mile away.

There are all these questions straight people ask me, when they realise I'm gay.

**Straight Person One**  When did you come out?

*He is about to answer, but is interrupted by the next question – and the next, and the next . . .*

**Straight Person Two**  When did you know that you were gay?

**Straight Person Three**  What did your dad say?

**Straight Person Four**  What did your mum say?

**Straight Person Five**  What did your friends say?

**Straight Person Four**  Did you lose any friends?

**Straight Person Two**  When did you get your first boyfriend?

**Straight Person One**  When was your first kiss?

**Straight Person Five**  How did you know the first guy you kissed was gay?

**Straight Person Three**  How do you meet other gay people?

**Straight Person One**  Do you go to gay bars?

**Straight Person Two**    Do you *like* gay bars?

**Straight Person Five**    Are you a Catholic?

**Straight Person Four**    Can you be a Catholic and gay?

**Seán**    This is every conversation I have at night clubs when there's someone that's never met a gay before.

**Straight Person One**    Do you like Diana Ross?

**Seán**    OF COURSE I like Diana Ross!

I do wear my sexuality on my sleeve. And a lot of people are like –

**Straight Person Five**    Why do you wear your sexuality on your sleeve? You don't *have* to, you know.

**Seán**    Yes – but I *want* to.

I want people to know there's a gay in the room.


**2009–2014**

*Pride.* **Mary** *addresses the crowd.*

**Mary**    Happy Gay Christmas! Are you having a good Pride?

*Cheers.*

**Mary**    Let's hear you make a bit of noise!

*More cheers.*

**Chorus**    June, 2009.

**Mary**    You know, the Government doesn't want you making noise.

*Boos.*

**Mary**    The Government thinks it can keep you quiet . . .

*Boos.*

**Mary**    And the thing it's offering to keep you quiet is called 'civil partnership' . . .

*She produces a copy of the Civil Partnership Bill.*

**Mary**    This is the Civil Partnership Bill, that GLEN is supporting.

*A frisson in the crowd.*

**Mary**    Civil partnership will officially make us second-class citizens in the eyes of the law. We don't want a lesser status – we want *equality*! Let's tell the government, and GLEN – this is what we think of your Civil Partnership Bill!

*She rips up the bill to raucous cheers.* **William** *and* **John** *look on in dismay. They turn on* **Siobhán**.

**William**    What the hell is going on?

**Siobhán**    We're not going to accept Apartheid for lesbians and gays.

**William**    We *are* unequal. That's the status quo that we're trying to change. This bill will give us greater equality.

**John**    How can you be against something that will make our lives better?

**Siobhán**    You don't speak for the community!

**John**    You don't have the right to tear down what we're doing!

**Siobhán**    Don't you get it? Incrementalism isn't enough any more.

**William**    What if the politicians see this and pull their support?

**Siobhán**    Maybe they'll see this and think they have to go further!

**Chorus**    July, 2010.

**Newsreader**   The Civil Partnership Bill has completed all stages in the Oireachtas and will become law as soon as it is signed by the President. The first civil partnership ceremonies are likely to be held early next year.

**William** (*with* **John**)   We did it.

**John**   Oh thank God.

*They hug. Separately:*

**Mary** (*with* **Siobhán**, *disheartened*)   They've won.

**Siobhán** (*resolute*)   So have we.

*The two pairs remain separate for the rest of the scene.*

**William**   But it's not over.

**John**   What's next?

**William**   I want to get married.

**Siobhán**   This should open the door to marriage.

**Mary**   What if it closes it? What if people now say, 'the gays have enough'.

**Siobhán** (*worrying*)   What if it's the gays who say that?

**Chorus**   July, 2012.

**Newsreader**   The Government has announced its intention to establish a 'Constitutional Convention' of ordinary citizens to consider the topic of same-sex marriage.

**John** (*with* **William**)   Ah for fuck's sake.

**Mary** (*with* **Siobhán**)   They're passing the buck.

**William**   Kicking it into the long grass . . .

**Siobhán**   It's just typical of Irish politics.

**Chorus**   April, 2013.

**Newsreader**   The constitutional convention has voted overwhelmingly in favour of extending marriage rights to same-sex couples.

**Mary**   I knew it!

**John**   I said it all along.

**Siobhán**   The power of democracy!

**William**   Trust the citizens!

**Chorus**   November, 2013.

**Newsreader**   The Government has announced that a referendum to allow same-sex marriage will be held the year after next.

**William** *and* **Siobhán** – *separate on stage – fall quiet.*

**Mary** (*with* **Siobhán**)   What's wrong?

**John** (*with* **William**)   What's up?

**Siobhán**   This is bigger than anything we've done . . .

**William**   This is a popular vote. We could lose it . . .

**Mary**   So what –

**John**   What do you mean –

**Siobhán**   We're going to have to . . .

**William**   We're going to have to work . . .

**Mary**   Oh no, you don't mean –

**John**   No *way* –

*The two pairs bump into each other again – awkward 'Hi!'s all round.*


### The Yes Equality Office – November, 2014

*A busy office.*

**Chorus**   November, 2014. Days to go: 180.

**William**   Let's get started.

**Siobhán**    First things first – what are we going to call this – the campaign?

**Mary**    What about 'Marriage Equality Now!'?

**John**    Too strident.

**Mary**    Leave off the lesbian clichés, will you.

**John**    We're starting a campaign to *persuade* people and you already want to turn it into a protest.

**Mary**    You know, you're right – what about 'Marriage Equality, *Please, Sir*'?

**William** (*intervening*)    The Gay and Lesbian Campaign for Marriage Equality –

**Siobhán**    That's too like GLEN.

**Mary**    The Campaign for Marriage Equality –

**John**    That's too like Marriage Equality.

**William**    The Campaign for Gay Marriage –

**Mary**    It's not 'gay marriage'.

**William** (*correcting himself*)    Gay and *lesbian* marriage –

**Siobhán**    It's just *marriage*.

**John**    For gays and lesbians.

**Mary**    For *everyone*. We already have '*gay* marriage' – that's what civil partnership is – similar, but different. And when we win this, there won't *be* 'gay marriage', any more. There'll just be marriage.

**John**    Not in the Church, there won't.

**Siobhán** (*impatient*)    *Civil* marriage, obviously.

**William** (*tentative*)    The Campaign for Civil Marriage Equality . . .

**John**    It's awfully clunky.

**William**    But clear.

**Mary**    It does what it says on the tin.

**William**    Okay, that's a working title, at least. What's next?

**Chorus**    Days to go: 179.

*The morning meeting, again.*

**Siobhán**    Okay: Advertising.

**Mary**    Social media's clearly going to be a huge force.

**William**    That's what they say every election. The old ways are the best ways.

**Siobhán**    We're already getting traction on Facebook.

**John**    How many likes?

**Mary** (*she checks*)    Em, seven. But we only launched it this morning.

**William**    Posters – they're the key.

**Mary**    Posters are so hackneyed. Does anybody even look at them?

**John**    In Ireland, political campaigns have posters. No posters – no credibility.

**Siobhán**    We can't *afford* posters!

**William**    We'll have to borrow.

**Siobhán**    Against what?

**William**    Against the money we're going to fundraise . . .

**Chorus**    Days to go: 178.

**William**    Okay – logistics. We'll need t-shirts . . .

**Siobhán**    High-vis vests.

**John** (*incredulous*)    High-vis vests?

**Siobhán**    For canvassing at night.

**Mary**   How naff!

**William**   And we'll need badges.

**Siobhán**   How many?

**William**   Ten thousand? For now.

**Mary**   Ten *thousand*? Are you insane?

**Siobhán**   This is going to be a ground war. We're going to need armies of canvassers in the trenches.

**Mary**   We're at 80 per cent in the polls!

**William**   And we have to convert that opinion into facts on the ground.

**John**   That's what publicity is for.

**Mary**   And marches.

**William**   The time for marching is over.

**Mary** (*exasperated*)   What, then?

**William**   A mass national canvass.

**John**   We have to be careful what we ask people to do.

**Mary**   You expect the community to come out – literally – to every house in the country?

**Siobhán**   That's what this might take.

**Mary**   Asking for their *approval*?

**William**   That's what this *is*. There's no way around that now.

**Chorus** (*with growing urgency*)   Days to go: 177.

**Siobhán**   Imagery: posters, ad campaigns, whatever – what's *on* them?

**John**   Families.

**Mary**   Gay people and their children?

**John**   No – their wider families – gay people amongst their families.

**Mary** (*sarcastic*)   Gay people with straight people – to reassure the straights.

**William**   We have the gay vote – it's the straights we're after.

**Siobhán**   And what about gay couples with their children?

**John**   Women, maybe – but no gay dads.

**Mary** (*outraged*)   Why not?

**William**   It scares people.

**Mary**   Oh, so because we can't afford to 'scare' the heterosexuals, we have to whitewash everything . . .

**William**   We have to win hearts and minds, first.

**Siobhán**   And we have to start with the hearts and minds of our own community!

**Chorus** (*frantic*)   Days to go: 176.

**William**   This isn't working.

**Siobhán**   We've never done this before.

**William**   We're campaigning for a public vote to legalise gay marriage – *nobody*'s ever done this before.

**Siobhán**   People have won referenda before . . .

**John**   Referend*ums*.

**Mary**   What?

**John**   The plural of referendum – it's referend*ums*.

**Mary**   It's referend*a*. Like memorandum – memorand*a*.

**John**   It's modern English –

**Mary**   It's *Latin*.

**John**   It's a Latin gerund – which doesn't take a plural –

**Mary**   Exactly.

**John**   But its use in this sense is a modern English innovation – so it takes a simple English plural.

**Mary**   Christ you're such a pedant. Obsessing about a word.

**John**   Oh now *I'm* the one obsessing about a word?

**William**   For Christ's sake, stop it!

For thirty years we have been working towards this. And we've made progress – incremental, but *consistent*. Decriminalisation . . . Equality legislation . . . Civil partnership . . . Each of them a gain. But this is different. This is the first time we're working on a campaign that could make things *worse* for our people. Because if we mobilise the community to campaign for this, and we lose, that won't be merely a political setback, it will be a punch in the face to every gay and lesbian in the country. For the first time, our countrymen, our fellow citizens will be saying, 'we've *thought* about this, and – no, you're not good enough'. If we can't pull together and put our disagreements behind us, that's what's ahead.

*Beat.*

**Siobhán**   We need help.


**Jane's Story**

**Jane** *steps forward. She is in her forties, from Cork.*

**Jane**   There was a bar, Loafers, in Cork . . . On Thursday nights . . . That was the spot – the only spot in Cork . . .

From where I lived, Loafers was on the left-hand side of Douglas Street. So I walked along the right-hand side . . . And I walked from one end of Douglas Street to the other end . . . and back up . . . and back down . . . and back up . . . and went home. And I did that about four different evenings. And eventually I went in.

I told my two closest friends. I said,

(*To* **Mary** *and* **Susan**.) If you ever meet my mother and she says

**Jane's Mother** (*to* **Mary** *and* **Susan**)   Oh, and you were out with Jane on Thursday night!

**Mary** (*to* **Jane's Mother**)   Em –

**Susan** (*to* **Jane's Mother**)   Oh –

**Jane**   You fucking *were*!

**Mary** (*dissembling*)   I was. Oh it was lovely.

**Susan** (*shifty*)   I was. Sure it was great.

**Jane**   So Thursday was the night I would go out and I would use them as the buffers . . . And that went on for about three years . . . It was as if 75 per cent of myself was consistently hidden. In hindsight, I hadn't really come out to myself.

And then I met someone, and fell madly in love . . . I was living at home but like, I used to stay in her house one or two nights of the week – and I would be back home in the morning at seven, and I'd crawl up the stairs into bed before my father would call me at quarter to eight –

**Jane's Dad**   Jane! Time to get up for work!

**Jane** (*faking a yawn*)   Coming!

(*To audience*.) But then my younger brother overheard me on a phone call, and while I was at work that day . . .

**Jane's Kid Brother**   Mam! Mam!

**Jane's Mum**   What is it for God's sake?

**Jane's Kid Brother**   Why was Jane telling someone called Nuala that she loves her?

**Jane**   So my sister phoned me, and I came home. And Mum was at the sink, mashing potatoes, and she was bawling crying into the potatoes. And she walked off upstairs. And I decided, right, we are having this out, now, for once and for all. So I followed her into her bedroom.

**Jane**'s **Mum**    Is it true?

**Jane**    Is *what* true, Mum?

(*To audience.*) I was like . . . just say . . . a word . . . and we will go from there.

**Jane**'s **Mum** (*with difficulty*)    That you are actually . . . going out with . . . this Nuala one . . .

**Jane**    I am, Mum.

**Jane**'s **Mum**    That you are actually one of them . . .

**Jane**    There's nothing I can do about it, Mum.

**Jane**'s **Mum**    What did we ever do wrong?

**Jane** (*crying*)    I'm so sorry I am disappointing you . . .

**Jane**'s **Mum** (*crying*)    I can't understand . . .

**Jane** (*to audience*)    This went on for about three-quarters of an hour . . . And, in the middle of all this, I completely forgot about my father.

**Jane**'s **Dad** (*calling*)    I'm home!

**Jane**    And I heard the thump, thump, thump, up the stairs . . . And I came out of the bedroom, thinking, oh Jesus, if this is the rest of my life, I don't want it . . . And my father was standing outside the door. And I looked at him –

(*To her* **Dad**.) Dad –

*She collapses in tears. He wraps her in his arms as she cries.*

**Jane**    I'm so sorry.

**Jane**'s **Dad**    Sure you're my daughter. I will always love you.

**The Yes Equality Office – December 2014**

**Chorus**    Days to go: 150.

**Siobhán**    Can we have some attention please, everybody.

*They gather round.*

**William**    Frank here is a political analyst, a consultant . . . and a former general election candidate for Fianna Fáil –

*Snorts of derision.*

**William**    . . . which means that, unlike the rest of us, he has worked on national election campaigns – successful campaigns. He's offered to help. Frank –

**William** *leads a desultory welcoming applause as* **Frank** *stands up.*

**Frank**    Clap yourselves on the back. You're at 80 per cent in the polls. You have five months to go . . . You can't lose.

*They cheer.*

**Frank**    I want you to imagine a theatre . . . Imagine the Olympia in Dublin. (*He gestures out into the auditorium and they all turn to look at it.*) You are all on the stage, making your arguments to the stalls, to the balcony. But the theatre's practically empty. There are some people in the first few rows, but they're just the usual suspects – activists, academics, politicians, media. Right now you have 80 per cent support in this theatre . . . but there's almost nobody here.

Then, as we get closer to the vote, people start to take their seats – slowly, in dribs and drabs. And then, suddenly, in the final weeks, there's a clamour outside and the theatre fills. And every argument you've made before then, to the empty theatre – every argument you think you've won – is irrelevant. The real argument starts now. And the fact that you had 80 per cent in an opinion poll five months out counts for nothing. Because it was 80 per cent of fuck all.

The referendum to abolish the Seanad. Five *days* before the vote, the Yes side was at 66 per cent in the polls. They lost. The first Lisbon referendum: the Yes side was ahead by two to one. They lost. The first Nice referendum: ahead by two to one. They lost. Some of you may remember the divorce referendum, in 1995: the Yes side was at 72 per cent at one point – they ended up scraping through, by just 10,000 votes – that's just one family in every polling station.

**John**   But *every* political party is behind this. All the main NGOs. The unions. Charities. Sports bodies . . .

**Frank**   Votes don't come in bundles from parties, from NGOs, or sports clubs, or colleges. They come in ones. Every single vote represents an individual decision. Every single Yes voter has to be personally persuaded to make that decision . . .

Say two million people vote on the day . . . Maybe half a million are immovable conservatives – we're never going to win them. Half a million are die-hard liberals – they're already on our side. There's a million in the middle, and they might go either way. They're not following you on Twitter, they're not your friends on Facebook, they don't even know this is *on*, yet. *They*'re your target audience.

You're in a bubble. A gay bubble. A liberal bubble. A political bubble. A media bubble. A middle-class bubble. A Dublin bubble. Do not for a minute think that the preferences of those inside this bubble reflect the intentions of those outside.

### Canvassing

**Gill** *stands apart: he is in Roscommon, the others elsewhere. The others always canvass in pairs.*

**Gill** (*to audience*)   They told us: never go canvassing on your own.

**Female Canvasser** (*at a door, nervous*)   Hello. We're canvassing for –

**Dublin Woman**   We don't want politicians round here with your lies and your water charges –

**Female Canvasser**   We're not politicians!

**Male Canvasser**   We're the gays.

**Female Canvasser**   And the lesbians.

**Dublin Woman**   The gays?

**Female Canvasser**   There's a referendum coming up . . .

**Male Canvasser**   For gay marriage!

*A neighbour shouts over.*

**Dublin Neighbour**   Run those politicians out of here, Louise, they'll bring no good.

**Dublin Woman** (*shouting back*)   It's not politicians, Jackie – it's the queers – they want to get married.

**Dublin Neighbour**   Ah bloody great! I'd love our Johnny to get married. Send 'em over here.

**Gill**   But in Roscommon, we have a very small amount of canvassers. Time is ticking.

**Canvasser Betty** (*at a door*)   Hello Máire.

**Betty's Neighbour** (*neighbourly*)   Oh, Betty! What are you –

**Canvasser Betty**   I'm canvassing for a Yes vote in the marriage equality referendum.

**Betty's Neighbour**   Oh! But why are *you* involved in this, Betty?

**Canvasser Betty**   Well . . . my Eoghan is gay, you know, Máire.

**Betty's Neighbour**   Oh my God! I'm so sorry! When was he diagnosed?

**Gill**   So I come to this estate. It's a friendly estate – I have friends in here. I'll do an hour, I think – get a hundred houses done – that could be, maybe, sixty more 'Yes' votes. So I put on my t-shirt – my armour – and I start knocking on doors . . .

(*At a door.*) My name is Gill, Gill Murphy. I'm from just down the road there . . . There's a vote coming up at the end of the month, for . . . marriage equality . . . And I hope you'll support it.

**Gill**'s **Neighbour**   Grand so, sure I know you to see, Gill. I'll have a think about that, now.

**Gill** (*to audience*)   And it's going well, at most of the doors . . . But because I'm on my own, every door I come to, it's like coming out, again and again. And because they're strangers, I can't know what to expect.

**Female Canvasser** (*at a door*)   Hello. We're canvassing for a Yes –

**Mickey Woman** (*shocked*)   You want me to vote to allow some man put his mickey in another fella's bottom . . .?

**Male Canvasser**   Well . . . No, actually – we can do that already.

**Female Canvasser** (*at another door*)   We're canvassing for a –

**Sympathetic Woman**   Of course I'll vote Yes –

*The* **Female Canvasser** *lights up with relief.*

**Sympathetic Woman**   sure it's not your own fault.

**Male Canvasser** (*at another door*)   Hello. We're canvassing for a Yes vote –

**Pissed-Off Man**   Ah would you *fuck off* with your same-sex marriage.

**Gill**   And it is like exposing myself, like a raw nerve . . .

**Female Canvasser** (*at another door*)   Hi. We're canvassing for –

**Ignorant Man**   You would be wanting dogs to marry cats next.

**Male Canvasser** (*at another door*)   Hello –

**Paranoid Man**   Get away from my door – there are kids in the house!

**Gill**   I get about three-quarters of the way through the estate and then I run back to my car and I rip off my Yes Equality t-shirt and . . . I just start crying.

**Female Canvasser** (*at another door*)   Hi. We're –

**Jesus Man**   Jesus didn't nail himself to the cross for the queers to go around and defy the word of God.

**Male Canvasser** (*at another door*)   We're –

**Butcher Woman**   You are only like animals, just fit for the slaughterhouse.

**Female Canvasser** (*at another door*)   Hi –

**Nazi Man**   They didn't build enough concentration camps for the likes of ye.

**Male Canvasser** (*at another door*)   We're canvassing for the marriage equality referendum.

**Bachelor Man**   Oh, sorry, no – I'm a bachelor.

*Puzzled beat.*

**Gill**   And that's when this becomes *real* to me . . . That's when I realise that I am not just doing this because everyone is doing it, because it's a 'thing' . . . I am doing it because it matters to *me* . . . But it is *hard* . . . Because it is like taking a cheese grater, and rubbing it up and down myself.

**Female Canvasser** (*at another door*)   We're canvassing with Yes Equality for the marriage equality referendum.

**Father**   Oh, well, I'll be voting 'No'.

**Female Canvasser** (*disappointed*)    Oh!

**Father**    No offence, like – I just don't see how it affects me or my family.

*A young woman emerges behind him.*

**Father** (*proudly*)    Sure three of my four daughters are married already. We've two grandchildren, more on the way probably.

**Female Canvasser**    Well it could affect your grandchildren – in the future . . .

**Father**    Sure that's ages away. Nothing against you, now, just it's got nothing to do with me.

*His daughter appears.*

**Daughter**    Dad –

*Beat.*

It has got to do with you.

*She starts to get upset.*

**Father**    What do you mean, love?

*The* **Canvassers** *start to click.*

**Daughter**    It *has* got to do with you, Dad.

**Father**    But how could it? Sure I've just the four of you, and the other three are married already, and you're –

**Male Canvasser** (*retreating*)    Maybe we'll leave you and your daughter to talk about it . . .

**Female Canvasser**    We might call back later.


**The Yes Equality Office – Early March, 2015**

**Chorus**    Days to go: 80.

**Frank** *approaches the others.*

**Frank** (*worried*)    I have the focus group results – the middle-aged men.

**William**    And?

**Frank**    Men aged between forty and sixty are a *soft* Yes. They haven't thought about it too much, but they see no harm in it. So we showed them the arguments that have been made internationally against gay marriage –

**Mary**    Such as?

**Frank**    Such as . . . 'Civil partnership should be sufficient' . . . And . . . the arguments about . . . children . . .

**Mary**    Children?

**William**    That children need a mother and father, that –

**Siobhán**    That gay men can't be trusted around children.

**Frank**    Yes.

**Mary**    It's 2015!

**John**    Do we *still* have to fight this?

**Siobhán**    Isn't it marginal enough to ignore it?

**Frank**    It's not marginal.

**John**    It's mainstream?

**Frank**    It's no longer as flagrant as it was. But it's easily implied. They just have to talk about 'mothers' – people get the picture.

**John**    The picture of two men with a child.

**Frank**    When our focus group of middle-aged men were exposed to this kind of material, they swung back to the No side. So that's what the No campaign is going to try and do.

**Mary**    So how do we fight it?

**Frank**    I don't know.

**Julie's Story**

**Julie** *steps forward. She is a Dub in her twenties or early thirties.*

**Julie**  I was having sex with boys from the age of . . . oh . . . twelve on. And any time I was with a fella, I was absolutely off my head. I was sniffing aerosols and everything. And it was all around that feeling of not belonging, feeling like I was an alien, a feeling like I was somehow looking down at myself in a life that wasn't mine . . . As a twelve-year-old, that, that was a very strong feeling.

So I tried to hang myself. I left notes to my Ma, to my sister, to my friend. There was one of them old-fashioned towelling robes – a large man's one of them – and I took the cord off that and tied it to the top of the built-in wardrobe. But the cord snapped.

Eventually, when I was in college, I met a girl – my first girlfriend . . . I told my Ma. She said –

**Julie's Ma**  I don't care if you ride a donkey, once it treats you right.

**Julie**  Then, I was texting my friend Darren, to tell him I'd introduced the bird to my Ma, and I went down through my numbers, to D, then Darren, and hit send . . . And then I got a call off . . .

*Her phone rings.*

**Julie** (*into phone, surprised*)  Da!

**Julie's Da**  Julie, eh –

**Julie**  Yeh?

**Julie's Da** (*worried*)  I just got a text there from you . . .

**Julie**  And so we went up and he met the girlfriend and I thought he had a big problem with it all . . . but he just didn't like *her*.

I was butch as a child, sporty. I can remember being young and having my nails painted, and sitting there and looking down and feeling like it was a lie . . . If I was getting dressed up to go out, I felt like I was a drag queen. And then when I came out, it was like everything made sense to me. It was like my femininity was my own. It wasn't for men. It wasn't for this life I was *supposed* to lead . . . I was, like, okay, now I can be me.

## The Yes Equality Office – Early April, 2015

**Chorus**    Days to go: 50.

**Frank** *assembles the team for a briefing and draws three concentric circles on a whiteboard (or uses some other device to illustrate or embody the circles).*

**Frank**    I want you to imagine three circles. This one – the inner one – is 'me and mine' – the voter's immediate family. The next one is extended family, friends, contacts generally. The outer circle is 'others out there' – that's where everybody else is – remote from me and my life.

People who have gay and lesbian people inside their inner circle – me and mine – are overwhelmingly in favour of marriage equality. But most people don't have gays in their inner circle. For the million in the middle, gay and lesbian people are still 'others out there'.

The gay marriage movement in America lost twelve State votes on marriage equality before they began to win. Why? Because their opponents convinced voters that gays and lesbians were 'others out there' – people who were trying to force change on them – change that could pose a threat to their own families – to 'me and mine'. The movement learned that to win, they had to move gay and lesbian issues from 'others out there' in towards 'me and mine'. So here's the question: how do *we* do that?

**Mary**    This is like when you go to a social media training, and they draw all those circles on the whiteboard – except they're overlapping. 'Networks', they call them.

**John**    The stories people are sharing on social media – it's heartbreaking.

**Frank** (*impatient*)    Fucking social media! How many times do I have to say it? This campaign will *not* be won on the internet! The million in the middle are not on Twitter!

**Mary**    But this is how social media works . . . Say, John's friend – I don't know him – he's 'others out there'. And then he posts something, and John likes it, and John's a friend of mine, so when he likes it, I get to see it, and then *I* like it . . . And so John's friend moves from 'others out there' into the middle circle . . . Social media does what you're talking about . . .

**Frank**    But the *real* world! How do we replicate that in the *real* world?

**Siobhán** (*inspired*)    By doing what people are doing on Facebook. Telling stories . . . Every time someone tells a personal story – on Facebook, in the media, to a meeting, at a door – they move from 'others out there' in towards their listeners.

**William** (*teasing it out*)    I saw a news report during the Scottish independence referendum . . . There was a woman standing on a corner, in Inverness, canvassing. And she had a homemade sign hung around her neck. And it said, 'I'm voting yes – ask me why.'

**Frank**    That's it! That's what we're missing!

**Siobhán**    What?

**Frank**    'I'm voting yes – *ask me why*.' I'm not going to lecture you, or hector you. I'm not going to guilt you. I'm not even going to try and persuade you. I'm just going to tell you my story, if you'd like to hear it.

**John**   So not only are we asking our people to knock on doors and come out to strangers – we're also going to ask them to tell their life stories?

**Frank**   Do you want to *win*? Because you're not going to win by winning the argument. You're going to win by making people cry.

### Fr Joe's Story

**Fr Joe** *steps forward. He is a native Irish speaker.*

**Fr Joe**   Every morning I put up a daily prayer . . . on my Facebook page. And one morning there is an invitation in my Facebook to attend a kind of little discussion group on the referendum. In a community centre in the parish. 'You are invited along' – you know the way . . . And I just click, 'Yes, I'll attend' . . . It's from the 'Yes' side.

*His mobile phone rings in his pocket.*

**Fr Joe** (*to audience*)   Sorry.

(*To phone.*) Hello?

**Raidió Na Gaeltachta**   Is that Fr Joe?

**Fr Joe**   It is.

**Raidió Na Gaeltachta**   This is Raidió na Gaeltachta. There's a Fr Joe here on Facebook says he's attending a Yes event . . . Is that you?

**Fr Joe** (*bemused*)   I suppose it is me.

**Raidió Na Gaeltachta**   Would you come on air and have a bit of a chat about it?

**Fr Joe**   Oh. Well . . . I suppose I would.

*The phone rings again.*

**Fr Joe**   Hello?

**Cork 96FM**   Fr Joe?

**Fr Joe**   Yes.

**Cork 96FM**   This is Cork 96FM. There's a comment up here in Facebook –

**Fr Joe**   That's me.

**Cork 96FM**   Would you like to come on air and –

**Fr Joe** (*not so comfortable*)   Well, I suppose –

*The phone rings again.*

**Fr Joe** (*tentatively*)   Hello?

**BBC Radio**   I'm looking for a Fr Joe – the Cork priest?

**Fr Joe**   Ye-es . . .

**BBC Radio**   Ah, excellent. I'm calling from the BBC –

**Fr Joe** (*panicked*)   It was just a comment on –

*The phone rings again.*

**Fr Joe** (*alarmed*)   Yes?

**German Radio**   Hallo. This is Deutschlandfunk – the national broadcaster of Germany. I am looking for the Irish priest who is with the gays –

**Fr Joe** *panics and hangs up. He breathes heavily.*

*The phone rings again. He looks at it, nervously, but recognises the number this time. He answers.*

**Fr Joe** (*warily*)   Hello, Bishop.

**Bishop** (*avuncular*)   Ah, Fr Joe . . . Listen, what's this about you going on the radio, Joe? Were you on about the referendum?

**Fr Joe**   Eh, yes, Bishop. I was on Raidió na Gaeltachta this morning.

**Bishop**   And saying you're thinking of voting Yes?

**Fr Joe**   That's right, Bishop.

**Bishop** (*kindly*)   But *I* am voting No, Joe. All the bishops are saying to vote No.

**Fr Joe**   Yes, Bishop.

**Bishop**   I think you should reflect on it a little more, Joe.

**Fr Joe** (*troubled*)   I will, Bishop.

**Bishop**   *Pray* about it . . . We'll talk about it again. I'll call you.

**Fr Joe** *hangs up.*

**Fr Joe**   So I reflect on it, more. And I pray . . . And in the meantime, I go along to the little meeting, the one on Facebook. There are about fifteen or twenty people there. And a local woman speaks, an older woman, Katherine, and her son, Niall.

### Katherine's Story

**Katherine** *steps forward, with* **Niall,** *her son. She is in her fifties or older, from West Cork.* **Niall** *is in his twenties.* **Fr Joe** *watches them.*

**Katherine**   My name is Katherine. We left the island when I was ten years of age . . . I have – I had four brothers and two sisters . . . I go to mass seven days a week. I never miss, the whole year. I pray the rosary last thing at night. And the first thing I do when I open my eyes in the morning, before I get out of bed, I thank God for another day, and tell him to look after my kids . . . Niall is my oldest, he'll be graduating in April – he'll be a doctor then –

(*With mammy pride.*) he's going to be a cardiologist . . .

**Niall**   My earliest memory of sexuality – or of me being maybe slightly a wee bit different – was that, very early on, I had a big interest in Irish dancing.

**Katherine**    My brother, Tony, moved to the city to work. And he met a very nice girl from Kinsale, and got married. But the day he got married . . . He was crying away that day . . . And my mother said to me, why is he – Ah, I says, he is just . . . happy and all. And then he took sick with depression . . . He had a nervous breakdown and he had to be hospitalised. And one day, when he was recovering, he said to me –

**Tony**    Katherine, I have something to tell you.

**Katherine**    Oh.

**Tony**    I'm gay.

That's why I'm sick. Because I'm holding it back for so long.

**Katherine**    You are my brother, Tony. It doesn't matter to me whether you are Black or white or what you are.

(*Hesitant.*) I'm sure Mam and Dad and the rest of the family will . . . feel the same.

**Niall** (*to audience*)    Uncle Tony's coming out gave me the opportunity to suss out how my family felt about things. So Mum told him she didn't care . . . but there were little things, like when he was going to come and stay with us, and they were, like –

**Katherine's Husband**    Well we can't have two men sharing a bed under this roof, with the kids . . .

**Niall**    When I went to bed at night, I would pray until I fell sleep. I would pray that I would wake up and wouldn't be gay. It was the last thing that went through my head every night. And then, when I woke up, the first thing I would think would be, oh – I'm still gay.

**Katherine**    I knew from an early age, you know, Niall was gay. I went to my local doctor –

**Doctor**    Ah, Katherine.

**Katherine**    Doctor – I think my Niall is gay.

**Doctor**   How old is Niall now, Katherine.

**Katherine**   Three.

**Niall**   When I was nineteen, I started going up to Dublin, and I started having encounters –

(*Off his mother's reaction.*) eh, a relationship – in Dublin. But I had also been dating girls. I thought, 'this is what is expected of me' – to have a normal life and a wife and kids . . . There was one girl I dated and, later on, she said –

**Girl**   Yeah, *loads* of people thought you were gay . . . but I just thought it was your Cork accent.

**Katherine**   Tony, my brother, recovered. His marriage was over, of course – I felt sorry for her – she was broken-hearted . . . He met a man. And they lived together for ten years, and they were happy. But then they broke up, and he took this very, very bad. He just went down and down and down. And then a friend of his – a gay friend – took his own life. And one day Tony said to me –

**Tony**   I'm not going to work anymore, Katherine. I can't cope with it.

**Katherine**   And he started staying in the house . . . He locked the door, he wouldn't let nobody in . . . I think really what got to Tony was . . . was some of our family disowned him, some of our brothers and sisters . . . His own twin brother as well . . .

And then – a Tuesday evening – I'm hanging a wash on the line and my daughter phones, and she says –

**Katherine's Daughter**   Ma, I just got a call – There's something wrong with Tony . . .

**Katherine**   When we get there, the guards are there . . . and the doctor is just leaving . . . And the doctor says –

**Doctor**   Don't go in, Katherine.

**Katherine**   But nobody is going to hold me back from my baby brother. So I go in, anyway, and –

(*Crying, now.*) Tony is – He is lying –

(*She can't describe it.*) And I lift him up into my arms and I shake him and I say, 'Wake up, Tony, you can't do this to us' – And somebody lifts me off – And I go outside and I roar my head off and I –

(*Shouting, crying.*) This is *your* fault, God – you *made* him this way.

### The Yes Equality Office – Late April, 2015

**Chorus**   Days to go: 30.

**Frank** *is pacing, agitated.*

**William**   What's wrong?

**Frank**   The Church.

**William** (*worried*)   Have they released something?

**Frank**   *That*'s what's worrying me. Why haven't they? What's going on?

**William**   We have our 'letter to the faithful' ready.

**Frank**   The Church will see it as an attack.

**William**   We can't ignore the faithful. The 'million in the middle' – you said it yourself.

**Siobhán**   Maybe the bishops have decided to keep their heads down on this one . . .

**Frank**   That'll be a first.

**Siobhán**   They've taken such a beating. Maybe they sense this one moving away from them.

**William**    Maybe they'll just release a statement . . . an advisory . . . maybe they'll encourage people to make up their own minds . . .

**Frank** (*with foreboding*)    We'll see.


### Fr Joe's Story

**Fr Joe**    The week after that meeting, where Katherine and Niall spoke, the Bishop visits.

**Bishop**    Fr Joe.

**Fr Joe**    Bishop.

**Bishop**    Maybe you could mention something at Mass, Joe . . . just to say that you're not against the Church's teaching.

**Fr Joe**    But Bishop – I'm not – I was *never* against the Church's teaching. I never said that I was.

**Bishop**    Well maybe if you could say that, Joseph, as part of your sermon, some day. Just to clear your name.

*Beat.*

**Fr Joe**    I only ever wanted to be a priest. Since I was maybe seven years old . . . Because I want to serve . . . to serve at the altar and to serve the people . . .

Sometimes, before locking up the church, in the evenings, I stop and say a last prayer . . . Sometimes there are no words at all – I am just moved by the Spirit . . . And there on my own, one night, in the darkness, it comes to me . . . There's a line in the Mass where the Lord says, 'Take this, all of you, and drink from it' . . . And he says '*all* of you'. He doesn't say, 'This is just for those of you who are straight'.


### The Yes Equality Office – Mid May, 2015

**Chorus**    Days to go: 12.

*The News comes on.*

**Newsreader**   The Catholic Archbishop of Armagh, Eamon Martin, has today called on people to 'reflect' and 'pray' before they vote in the marriage referendum.

**Archbishop** (*making statement*)   Openness to children who are born of the love and sexual relationship of their mother and father is an essential part of marriage . . . To interfere with the traditional definition of marriage is not a simple or trivial matter.

**Frank**   Fuck!

*He throws something at the telly.*

**Frank**   It's outrageous!

**Siobhán**   Frank –

**Frank** (*urgently*)   We have to take it to them.

**William**   Eh, Frank – we can't 'take it to them' –

**Frank**   They're too influential to ignore.

**Siobhán**   What do you / mean by 'take it to them'?

**William**   I didn't think it was / that bad at all.

**Frank**   It's bullshit. It's the tone, / the knowing tone.

**William**   But the tone was quite mild / and understated.

**Frank**   That's the point! It's politically brilliant. No threats. No hellfire and brimstone. It's a dog whistle. 'Not a simple or trivial matter.' Insinuating that your marriages – gay marriages – will somehow threaten children . . .

**William**   But this is precisely the argument we've been fighting all along.

**Frank**   But now it's been *legitimised*! This gives people permission to vote on their prejudice. We can't just sit back and take it.

**Siobhán** (*worried*)   What do you want / to do?

**Frank**   Come out hard. Strong. Quickly.

**William**   With –

**Frank**   A statement. Calling them out. Exposing their dog whistle. And then a litany – all of the abuse scandals. Throw it back at them. Ridicule them.

*He grabs paper and pen and starts to sketch it out.*

**Frank**   It needs to be out before the next News. Then a press conference. Tomorrow at midday. Somewhere iconic . . . Is there a decommissioned church we could use?

**William**   We can't / use a church!

**Siobhán**   Let's have a think / about this –

**Frank**   What's going on? Why aren't you angry? You should be spitting fire . . .

**William**   Welcome to *our* world.

**Siobhán**   Where have you been for the last forty years? The Catholic Church comes out against gay marriage – and that's a surprise?

**Frank**   We expected it. We feared it. But now we need to respond.

**Siobhán**   No!

**Frank** (*disbelieving*)   You're just going to suck it up?

**William**   That's exactly what we'll do. That's what we've always done.

**Siobhán**   They're the biggest, the most powerful non-governmental organisation in this country. And they would like nothing better than for us to turn this into a slagging match – drive it *up* the news agenda – draw *more* attention to what they've said – make them look more reasonable and us, less so . . .

**Frank**   We have to respond!

**William**    We'll say what we always say . . .

**Siobhán**    'We respect the Church's right to speak . . .'

**William**    'The Church is entitled to have a view . . .'

**Siobhán**    We *never* go bald-headed for the Church.

**William**    We've learnt that the hard way.

**Siobhán**    Over decades.

**Frank**    But your people –

**Siobhán**    Our people have been listening to the same offensive crap from the Church all their lives. They're almost immune to it. We're not going to risk our referendum strategy to take a shot at them now.

**William**    There may be a time to strike out – but this isn't it.

**Frank**    There's twelve days to go! What if we leave it too late?

**Siobhán**    The final polls are this weekend. Let's see what they say. *If* the polls show us losing  –

**William**    Then maybe it's time to attack.


**Gareth's Story**

**Gareth** *steps forward. He is in his early twenties. His mother,* **Selina**, *follows.*

**Gareth**    I had people telling me I was gay before I even told myself . . . The bullies in school, turns out they had a really good gaydar . . .

**Schoolboys** (*sing-song*)    Gareth is ga-ay! Gareth is ga-ay!

**Selina**    He was maybe thirteen at the time, and he came home and he was distressed. So I went down to see the principal.

(*To* **Principal**.) They are calling Gareth names, Principal, and writing it on the walls in the toilets . . .

**Schoolboys** (*sing-song*)   Gareth is ga-ay! Gareth is ga-ay!

**Principal** (*worried*)   Oh, what are they calling him, Mrs O'Brien?

**Selina**   They're calling him 'gay'.

**Principal** (*relieved*)   Oh Mrs O'Brien, don't worry about *that*! They don't mean Gareth is 'gay' as in 'homosexual' – they just mean he's not cool.

**Gareth**   So I made a decision, early on: I don't need those people in my life. Their opinions don't matter. They don't define me.

But still, I didn't know how to define myself . . .

*He picks up his guitar and checks the tuning.*

**Gareth**   There are no songs for guys singing about guys. Even gay pop stars, they don't sing about guys – they use female pronouns . . .

*He warms up on the guitar.*

**Gareth**   I knew I'd find it really difficult to go to a stranger's door and *ask* them to say, 'Yes', so that I can have the same rights as them . . . So I decided to record a YouTube video . . .

*He plays and sings the opening lines of the song 'Rude', by Magic.*

**Gareth**   This is a song about a guy asking his girlfriend's dad can he marry his daughter.

*He continues the song.*

**Gareth**   It's by the band Magic.

*He continues.*

**Gareth**   I decided to change it . . . So now it's about me, like, asking a nation can I get married at all . . .

(*Sings.*)    *Can I have your son for the rest of my life?*

*He continues the song.*


**The Yes Equality Office – Saturday, 17 May, Midnight**

*They are all intermittently checking their phones.*

**Chorus**    Days to go: 6 . . .

(*Looks at watch.*) 5.

**William**    It's midnight.

**Frank**    Nothing yet.

**Siobhán**    For fuck's sake.

**Mary** (*spotting a tweet*)    It's out!

**William** (*anxious*)    Well?

**Mary**    Hang on!

*They all try to get the* Sunday Independent *website up on their computers/phones.*

**Mary**    Oh Jesus.

*The others are all struggling with their devices.*

**Frank** (*impatient*)    What is it?

**Siobhán** (*overlapping*)    I can't / find it

**William** (*overlapping*)    This thing is too / slow

**Mary**    'Yes vote in freefall.'

*Beat.*

That's the headline.

*Deathly silence.*

**William**    But that's not possible –

**Siobhán**    The other polls –

**Mary** (*reading*)   'Support for same-sex marriage is in free fall – *down 13 points* in a month, an opinion poll has found. Only a *slim majority* now say they intend to vote Yes in the marriage referendum on Friday . . . The *sharp fall* in Yes support is evident across the urban/rural divide, among men and women and in *all* age groups . . . Only a minority of rural voters intend to vote Yes, down 14 points . . . And a minority of male voters say they will vote Yes – down 18 points . . .'

**William**   The Church.

**Mary**   The insinuations about children.

**Frank**   Perhaps.

**Siobhán**   What do we do now?

**Mary**   Go all out?

**John** *crashes in, suddenly, carrying the print edition.*

**John**   The fucking Sindo!

**William**   We've got it. Online.

**John**   Fucking 'free fall'. We're fucked.

**Siobhán**   We *can't* be fucked.

**John**   It's the final weekend. There's five days to the vote.

**Siobhán**   We still have a 'slim majority' –

**John**   It'll be gone by Friday. The momentum is all one way. We can't turn it around . . . We should have gone all out. We should have gone for them. We should never have sat here, taking it.

**Frank** *has been reading the article more closely.*

**Frank**   I don't think / we can come to that conclusion

**Mary**   This sends out a message. That it's *okay* to vote 'No'.

*Beat.*

We have done what we've been told. We have acted straight; we have silenced our more outspoken spokespeople; we have held in our anger; we have pretended to like some of our most vicious critics; we have pretended that there *isn't* a deep well of intolerance and hatred out there that needs to be called out. All that – and now we might *lose* this? It's time to fight back . . . It's time to stop pleading for the crumbs from the straight man's table.

**William**   But the Scottish example –

**John**   The Scots lost!

So much for their 'storytelling'.

**Frank**   We should keep faith with the strategy of the campaign.

**John**   This isn't just a 'campaign'. This isn't like a general election, or Seanad reform, or some other referendum. This is our lives. This is about whether our country wants us or not. And I am sick of having to pretend I fit in in order to make it easier for my country to include me.

If we lose this, you get to write a book about it, and you'll go on to the next campaign with your liberal credentials burnished . . . But this isn't a 'gig' for us. We – we have to *live* with it. Do you know what some of our people are doing this week? They're training youth workers to deal with suicide. Because they think, if this is *lost*, there'll be a spike . . .

**Frank** (*quietly*)   It's a trap.

**John**   You said it yourself a week ago – when the Church came out with its statement – it's time to fight back!

**Frank**   I was wrong. It was a trap then, and it's a trap now.

**Siobhán**   How do you / know that?

**Frank**   Look at the details of this poll: we've gone down – but the Nos have barely gone up. People aren't going from Yes to No – they're going from Yes to Don't Know. They're *confused.* The No arguments have succeeded in muddying the waters –

**John**    Which is why we should be fighting them, hard –

**Siobhán**    The more we fight back, the more the media will call us nasty . . .

**William**    The more we'll get defensive . . .

**Siobhán**    The more it'll look like the momentum is against us . . .

**Frank**    And the more we'll *scare* the undecideds . . . It's a vicious circle. The undecideds are trying to work out who they feel most comfortable with. The Church came out with its reasonable line – we have to sound just as reasonable. Which means keeping doing what we've done best all along – telling *stories.*


### Síofra's Story

**Síofra** *steps forward. She is in her twenties, from Longford.*

**Síofra**    There was a young fella, who played really well on the school GAA team, and he was in the Longford Leader one week. And I cut his picture out and I put it on my locker in school and I said to myself, now that's it – now I have a *name!* When I get asked, I'm going to say *his* name. Because everyone else had a name.

*Her classmates descend on her, boisterously.*

**Classmate One**    Who d'ye fancy, Síofra?

**Classmate Two**    Who's your fella, Síofra?

**Classmate One** (*confiding*)    I fancy Henry.

**Classmate Two**    Henry – he's a gobshite!

**Classmate One**    Fuck off you. With your Peadar and his potato head!

**Síofra**   As I went on through my teens, I got used to being invisible, to boys. I was never approached on nights out. And so I kind of settled with that. I busied myself with other things. It was lonely . . . The word 'lesbian' terrified me. It sounds like, you know, a bag of coffee . . . a lez-bean – like, what's that?

So then I'm leaving for a year, to go to college in Boston. And Mammy is helping me pack. And she asks me –

**Síofra**'s **Mammy**   Síofra, do you think . . . you might be . . . gay?

**Síofra** (*horrified*)   I don't know, Mammy . . .

(*Very uncertain.*) I might be . . .

(*To audience.*) Because I – I've no evidence. I just don't like guys.

And then I'm at this house party in Boston. And there's this girl, Jenny, and she's so intellectual, she goes on feminist marches, she's so confident . . . And she says to me –

**Boston Jenny**   Síofra, have you ever kissed a girl?

**Síofra** (*horrified*)   No.

**Boston Jenny**   Well, would you like to?

**Síofra** (*conflicted*)   Em . . . Maybe.

(*To audience.*) But in my mind I'm like, 'Yes, I would, absolutely, 100 per cent.' But I can't really get that out.

And then she just –

**Boston Jenny** *leans over and they kiss.*

**Síofra**   And I just suddenly feel at home.

And when I come home from America, I'm barely home a night and I'm going to the March for Marriage. And Daddy, Daddy doesn't understand *why* . . .

**Síofra's Daddy** (*to* **Síofra's Mammy**)   Why is – Why is she *doing* this to us? Why is she doing this to *herself*?

**Síofra**   I get very involved in the referendum campaign, in Dublin. I have everyone's ears blown off. But not once do I ever say that *I* have a stake in this. And then the Yes Equality bus is going to Longford and they ask me, will I go down with them. And suddenly it becomes very real . . .

When you let the cat out of the bag, normally – when you come out – it's containable – your friends know, your family, whoever you *choose* to tell. But when you let the cat out of the bag in rural Longford, the cat goes running off into the bog, and it doesn't come back.

And on my way down, on the bus, I ring Daddy, just to warn him, like – well, because he's going to hear about it anyway. And we arrive into the market square in Longford at twelve o'clock and . . . Daddy is standing there, waiting. And he comes up to me and . . . he asks me . . .

**Síofra's Daddy**   Síofra.

*Beat.*

Could I have one of the little colouredy badges you have.

*She gives him one, and he pins it on his jacket.*


### The Yes Equality Office – Thursday, 21 May

**Chorus**   Days to go: 1.

*The office is buzzing.* **Frank** *sits alone in a corner, studying something, brooding.* **Mary** *and* **John** *enter, excitedly.*

**Mary**   We've just handed out our five-hundred-*thousandth* badge!

**John**   The kids are trading them in schools.

**Siobhán**   Who took it?

**Mary**   A man . . . in his eighties.

**William**   We're at two to one in most of the polls.

**Siobhán**   We're going to do this.

**Frank** (*outburst*)   We can't rely on the polls!

**John**   But you're the pollster!

**Frank**   It's all about *turnout* now. How many Yes voters are looking at the polls and thinking, 'it's in the bag'? And how many of our voters have to make an *effort* to vote – students, say, who have to get on a bus tomorrow and go home? Well, how many of those might just be thinking, 'sure, there's no need'? And if it rains tomorrow and it's miserable, how many might look out the window and think, 'sure, it's safe anyway'.

*They are silent now, worried.*

*Lights up on a series of actors, elsewhere on stage. As he talks, the campaign staff get back to their individual tasks in the office, more sombre than before.*

**Martin**   I've been keeping in close contact with all of my friends, and keeping up to date with everything, listening to RTÉ all the time on the internet. And the closer it's been getting to the time, the more anxious I've been getting. If I was at home in Dublin I'd be out knocking on doors. But I just feel so out of the loop here, in Sydney. So I decide to book a ticket and come home . . .

**Jillian**   It feels hypocritical to not even make the effort to travel home to vote . . . So I ring into work sick, and off I go on the train from Leicester to Holyhead.

**Neil**   We've been away, in New York, too long to be allowed actually cast a vote, but we come back anyway.

**Tríona**   It costs me 1,500 Australian dollars, but I'm too afraid of the guilt I'll feel if it doesn't pass and I'd not done anything.

*In the office:*

**Siobhán**　Uh, has anyone been on Twitter?

**William**　Not in the last half hour.

**Siobhán**　There's a new hashtag –

**William**　Oh not another hashtag! We've been trying to concentrate the traffic on the official one!

**Siobhán**　This is different.

**William**　What is it?

**Siobhán**　'Home to vote.'

**Frank** (*overhearing*)　What?

**Siobhán**　Home to vote.

**Frank**　All one word?

**William**　It's a hashtag! They're *all* all one word.

**Frank**　Hash-tag?

**Mary**　Yes!

**Frank**　How do I do that again?

**John** *takes over at* **Frank***'s device.*

**John**　Here. Hashtag. Home. To. Vote.

**Tweeter One**　In Heathrow airport waiting for a flight to Cork to go #hometovote #MakeGráThelaw

**Tweeter Two**　#hometovote from London, weather amazing & all! #yesequality

**Tweeter Three**　A very busy Edinburgh to Dublin flight tonight with a lot of people going #hometovote

**Tweeter Four** (*taking a selfie*)　This is the scene on the London to Holyhead train as Irish abroad return #hometovote

**Tweeter Five**　Starting my trip from Goettingen to come #hometovote

**Tweeter Six**    Waking up in Slovakia. Can't wait to get #hometovote. @Ryanair get me home!!

**Tweeter Seven**    From New York to Limerick. I'm #hometovote #MakeGráTheLaw

**Tweeter Eight**    Never been so happy to be at an airport gate. LGA to PHL to DUB to YES. #hometovote

**Tweeter Nine**    Flew back yesterday from Nairobi to Cork #hometovote

**Tweeter Ten** (*taking a selfie*)    Going #hometovote from Mozambique can be tiring . . . So proud of my husband!

**Tweeter Eleven**    On my way #hometovote from Ethiopia! Wrecked tired, itching to vote!

**Sam**    The bus from London, on Thursday night, is packed. Everybody doing the same thing. People with rainbow t-shirts, banners . . . The rest of us spend the journey trying to make our own. Then we get to Holyhead, and the boat, and it's the same thing, hundreds of us, from London and across England and Wales, coming home to vote . . .

*At some point during the sequence, a woman starts to hum the melody 'She Moves Through the Fair'.*

**Frank** (*quietly*)    It's over.

**William**    But it's just some kids! How many can there be?

**Frank**    Hundreds, maybe –

**William**    That's not enough to make a difference!

**Siobhán**    You said it yourself! If the vote is slipping –

**Frank**    If *hundreds* of kids are coming home to vote, from London, from Boston, from fucking Sydney, then *thousands* of kids who are *already* home are going to get off their asses tomorrow to vote. And they'll drag their grannies with them. Our last fear was turnout. This clinches it.

**Sam**    And as we come towards the North Wall – and for all the years that I've been making this journey, I've always loved that moment, when the boat comes into the bay, and I can see home again – the texture of it, the greys of the sea and the sky and the piers – and we're up on deck, all of us, watching the city approaching – our city. And this girl starts to sing.

*The woman who has been humming now breaks into song.*

**Singer**
*My young love said to me, my mother won't mind*
*And my father won't slight you for your lack of kine,*
*And she stepped away from me and this she did say,*
*It will not be long love till our wedding day.*

*As she sings, the campaign staff clear the office out. And* **Victor** *steps forward, again.*

### Victor's Story

**Victor**    I had a stroke, just a few years ago, and I almost died, and I was unconscious three or four weeks. And then I started getting the use of my brain back again . . . and, gradually, after about twelve months, things started coming back . . . things would come into my head . . . things that I thought were gone forever. And one of them was being gay . . . I was coming down home on the bus from the hospital in Dublin. And there were the Yes posters everywhere. God, I said, that's an idea, I said – am I to 'come out' now, with the 'Yes' campaign on the move and all of this around the country? People might understand.

But, eh . . . they didn't understand. I had trouble with a couple of very close friends. One was . . . my brother . . .

**Victor's Brother**    This big secret you've had – why did you have to bring it out *now*?

**Victor**    He's been my best friend all my life, like.

**Victor's Brother**    What about the children? You're their uncle!

**Victor**    What *about* the children? I'm not one of them people that runs after kids!

**Victor's Brother**    I'm finished with you, now – I'm finished.

**Victor**    After I decided to come out, then I seen the gay people in the college. Jesus, I said, I would love to meet up with some of these. Because I never really met – Well, I didn't meet many more than one gay person – only Paddy. And that wasn't meetings, at all . . . I was checking on the college website and they said that they were having . . . a 'gay ball', they called it. Out in Ballybrit.

*Music starts.*

**Victor**    And I contact the secretary. I says

(*To Secretary.*) I have never been at a gay function of any description in my life.

**Secretary**    Well, we would love to have you, Victor. You'll be most welcome.

*The lights dim. A disco ball appears. Couples take to the floor as the music continues under* **Victor**.

**Victor**    There's a couple of hundred there . . . And they're dancing . . .

*A couple kisses.* **Victor** *marvels at them.*

**Victor**    And kissing . . . And I –

*One of them whisks him into a dance for a moment.*

**Victor**    I'm actually out dancing with them . . .

*They continue to dance and he stares at them.*

**Victor**    And I feel . . . I feel a great thrill, like, within me, being amongst them all. I feel . . . I don't . . . I never felt like this before.

*As the dance beat builds, the singer returns to her song, in time with the beat, the rest joining in.*

### Singer

*Last night she came to me, she came softly in*
*So softly she came that her feet made no din*
*As she laid her hand on me and this she did say*
*It will not be long, love, till our wedding day.*

*Curtain.*

# Afterword

Before this play, I knew Charlie Bird only as the veteran news journalist off the telly. Retired from RTÉ, and suddenly free to involve himself in political causes, Charlie had agreed to compère the launch event for the Yes Equality campaign – and then found himself doing more and more campaign events, all round the country. These events were different to the normal stuff of political campaigning – the kinds of events Charlie had spent a career reporting on. At their heart were very simple, intimate, honest acts of storytelling.

After the referendum, Charlie put a video camera in the car and went back around the country, recording these stories and more. He didn't know quite why he was doing this; he just knew this was a story that, despite the success of the referendum, remained to be fully told. He brought the idea of a book to Merrion Press and then a surprising idea occurred to him: could his interviews make a play? Charlie asked his old friend and colleague, Ed Mulhall, for any leads, and Ed put Charlie in touch with me. We met in a café on Dawson Street. Charlie handed me a sheaf of papers – the transcripts of his first batch of interviews (he was still doing them) – and then shifted anxiously in his seat while I looked at them. He didn't have to wait long. It took me about 60 seconds to see that this was the raw material of theatre. But, arresting though the individual stories were, they needed a spine to fuse them together. I suggested to Charlie that that spine might be provided by the story of the campaign itself, and so he added to his interview roll three of the key figures in that campaign: Gráinne Healy, Brian Sheehan and Noel Whelan. Their memoir of the campaign, *Ireland Says Yes*, gave me further detail; I drew on Una Mullally's oral history, *In the Name of Love*, for the deeper history of the movement, as well as on further interviews and archival research.

As these sources document, the story of the fight for gay rights – and eventually marriage equality – in Ireland is a long one, involving many organisations, many leaders, and many, many people. This telling of it reduces it to 90 minutes or so, with eight actors, and focusses on the final months. Accordingly, I've reduced the core narrative of the campaign to five fictionalised characters and two named organisations, GLEN and Marriage Equality. This is a play, not a history: it contains fact and fiction. The campaign strategies described, the political analysis cited and the personal stories – as well as all the best lines – are all the work of other people. The mistakes, over-simplifications and caricatures are my own. As always, the play has changed significantly from the first draft I handed to producer Pat Moylan and director Gerard Stembridge: they, as well as the casts of the productions of 2018 and 2019, have had a huge influence on the shape of the play.

In particular, the stories of Jenny Blake, Gavin and Sabina Brennan, Síona Cahill, June Hamill, Will Keane, Kathleen and Noel Sharkey, Steven Sharpe, Brian Sheehan and Nuala Ward are integral to the play, as well as those of Charlie's interviewees who preferred to remain anonymous. Other people whose words and insights informed the play, through either my own research or the sources already cited, include: Michael Cronin, Vivian Cummins, Oein DeBhairduin, Claire Goss, Mark Govern, Ursula Halligan, Ian Healy, Gerard Howlin, Breda Larkin, Anne Marie Lillis, Trudi Mc Donald, Rachel Morgan, Sharon Nolan, Colm O'Gorman, Mícheál Ó Ríordáín, Kathryn O Riordan, Niall O'Neill, Panti, Kieran Rose, Sharon Slater. The 'three circles' speech by the character of Frank is based on the account given in *Ireland Says Yes* of a presentation given to the Yes Equality leadership by Thalia Zepatos of Freedom to Marry. The tweets were by @debbiemoneill, @carceralcollapz, @dguilf, @naomiohreally, @jasonbyrnephd, @declanjhayes, @clareconboy, @belindamckeon, @cormac212, @g8rswmr and @clisare.

Colin Murphy